IMAGES
of Wales

CWM RHONDDA
FACH
TREHAFOD TO MAERDY

Cwm Rhondda That I Love

Some may long for golden sands
That stretch for miles and miles,
Some may long for foreign lands
And tropical green isles,
Some may long for yachts so fine,
For cruises on the sea,
But old Cwm Rhondda I love best,
This is the place for me

There are no sands or sunny isles
But steep hills scarred and old,
When bathed in summer's sunshine
. These green hills turn to gold;
There's freedom on the hill tops green
To romp and roam and run,
And you can hear a skylark's call
While lying in the sun.

There may be lovelier places,
There may be grander sights,
But look down in the evening
At the valley's twinkling lights-
When hills, like giant sentinels
Stand tall against the sky,
And bathed in silvery moonlight
The sleeping houses lie.

Chorus:
Cwm Rhondda, Cwm Rhondda,
Proud Valley I call home,
That like a magnet draws me back
Wherever I may roam.

Words and music by Hawys Glyn James,
former mayor of the Rhondda Valley.

IMAGES
of Wales

CWM RHONDDA FACH
TREHAFOD TO MAERDY

David Owen

TEMPUS

Acknowledgements

Thank you all for the wonderful stories and photographs relating to Cwm Rhondda Fach which have been given to me by the people of the villages. These have come from the first quarter of the nineteenth century through to the new millennium.

Our miners, our workers, our choirs, our scholars, our actors, our writers, our sportsmen, our movements of protest and reform, our 'characters', our passion for the community and comradeship all exist as proudly and as positively today as they have done for almost 200 years.

I sincerely thank everyone for their kindness and help. I dedicate this book to the people of Cwm Rhondda.

David Owen, author and archivist

Cydnabyddiaethau

Diolch i bawb o bobl y pentrefi sydd wedi cyfrannu storïau a lluniau am Gwm Rhondda Fach. Mae'r casgliad wedi dod o chwarter cyntaf y bedwaredd ganrif ar bymtheg hyd at y milflwydd newydd.

Mae ein glowyr, corau, ysgolheigion, awduron, chwaraewyr, mudiadau protest a diwygio, cymeriadau, cariad at fro a brawdgarwch yn bodoli gyda chymaint o falchder ac mor gadarnhaol heddiw ac y bu erioed am y 200 mlynedd diwethaf.

Rwy'n ddiolchgar i bawb am eu cymorth a charedigrwydd. Rwy'n cyflwyno'r llyfr yma i bobl Cwm Rhondda.

David Owen, awdur ac archifydd

First published 2003

Tempus Publishing Limited
The Mill, Brimscombe Port,
Stroud, Gloucestershire, GL5 2QG

British Library Cataloguing in Publication Data.
A catalogue record for this book is available from the British Library.

ISBN 0 7524 2687 7

typesetting and origination by Tempus Publishing Limited
printed in great britain by Midway Colour Print, Wiltshire

Contents

Preface

If the streets of London were paved with gold, then the streets of Cwm Rhondda (Rhondda Valley) were certainly paved with 'black gold' after coal was discovered and the pits were sunk. The 'coal rush' had begun. People flocked to the Rhondda Valley in their thousands in search of new jobs and a new way of life, bringing their families with them to begin mining the vast resources of the Valley.

My maternal grandfather came here from Llanberis, a village at the foot of Snowdon, bringing his family with him. Before coming to the Rhondda my mother had worked in the small café at the summit of Snowdon.

In 1910, my father migrated to Cwm Rhondda from the beautiful Llŷn Peninsula in Gwynedd. Before coming here he worked on a sailing ship taking a cargo of granite from Nantgwrtheyrn in Llŷn to small ports around the country. On one of these trips my father was wrongly accused of stealing a chicken and he was whipped. So, on reaching Port Talbot, he jumped ship and made his way over the mountains to Ferndale in the Rhondda Fach where his uncle William lived in Protheroe Street. Then he obtained work as a repairer in Ferndale No. 4 Pit.

At the beginning of the twentieth century, my husband's father left Cardigan to work as a carpenter with Mr Brown, the builder, in Ferndale, but after a few years he returned home.

In 1942, Glyn, my husband, left Llangrannog after serving his apprenticeship in Cardigan Foundry and came to work as a fitter in Tylorstown No. 9 Pit.

He clearly remembers the day he arrived in Cwm Rhondda. Dusk was falling as the train pulled out of the Blaengwynfi tunnel. Suddenly, the Penpych Mountain loomed before him, towering, formidable and gargantuan. He felt like an inhabitant of Liliput facing an immense Gulliver. Glyn was overwhelmed, frightened and lonely, and almost took the next train back to Cardigan. But he stayed.

Probably most families in the Rhondda would have fascinating and interesting tales to tell of how their grandparents and parents had migrated to our valley. Their stories would provide material for a very interesting book.

It is said that photographs are 'frozen fragments of time' and, like *Dr Who*'s Tardis, can transport us into another time and another era. For an older generation, long-forgotten memories return, while a younger generation have an opportunity to view the Rhondda of the past and compare it with the present.

Our thanks go to David Owen for his time, trouble and hard work in collecting these excellent photographs, for the information contained in this book and for bringing the past to life, for the past is our inheritance.

Rydym yn llongyfarch David Owen ar ei gasgliad o luniau arbennig a thrawiadol o fywyd yn ein cymunedau glofaol yn y gorffennol.

Glyn and Hawys James, former mayor and mayoress of the Rhondda

Foreword

This is David Owen's eighth volume of photographs depicting life in the Rhondda in the recent and the more distant past. He is to be praised for his diligence in seeking out such a varied collection, in that all aspects of life are represented.

While of great interest to those of us still living in Cwm Rhondda, the books are perhaps even more gratefully received by those 'expats' who have left the valleys. For older people the pictures evoke memories. For younger readers they provide historical and pictorial evidence of what life was like when 'King Coal' ruled the lives of everybody who lived in the mining villages.

In this book work and recreation are represented. The pits were the centres of employment and with their disappearance it is vital that records are kept of the hard conditions under which men earned their living. Education has always been of importance to the people of Rhondda and again it is fitting that so many items record school classes and activities. Sport also has its place with rugby, football, cricket and hockey being shown. Music (in the choir and brass band fields) and drama are included to show the importance of culture in the communities, and the prominence of religion in the history of Cwm Rhondda is represented here through the chapels and churches of the area.

Once again, our thanks go to David Owen. We are sure that this book will be as successful as his previous volumes.

Mair and Terry Williams

Rhagarweiniad

Dyma wythfed gyfrol o luniau yn adlewyrchu bywyd yn y Rhondda yn y gorffennol ac yn ddiweddar. Mae'n rhaid ei longyfarch am ei ddiwydrwydd yn hel casgliad mor amrywiol, ac fe adlewyrchir holl fywyd yr ardal ynddo.

O ddiddordeb i'r rhai ohonom sy'n byw o hyd yng Nghwm Rhondda, serch hynny efallai mae'r llyfrau o fwy o ddiddordeb i'r 'alltudion' sydd wedi gadael y cymoedd. I'r rhai henach mae'n hel atgofion. I'r ifanc mae'n darparu tystiolaeth hanesyddol ac mewn lluniau o fywyd yn ystod cyfnod 'Y Brenin Glo', oedd yn teyrnasu dros fywydau pobl oedd yn byw yn y pentrefi glofaol.

Cynrychiolir gwaith a hamdden yn y llyfr yma. Roedd y pyllau yn ganolfannau gwaith a gyda eu diflaniad mae'n allweddol bod cofnodion yn cael eu cadw am y cyflwr caled roedd dynion yn ennill eu bywoliaeth. Mae addysg wedi bod yn gonglfaen i bobl y Rhondda ac mae'n addas felly fod yna sôn am ddosbarthiadau a gweithgareddau ysgol. Roedd lle hefyd i chwaraeon gan gynnwys rygbi, pêl droed, criced a hoci. Cofnodir cerddoriaeth (ym meysydd y band pres a chôr) a drama, sy'n adlewyrchu pa mor bwysig oedd diwylliant yn y cymunedau a hefyd dylanwad crefyddol capeli ac eglwysi yn hanes Cwm Rhondda.

Unwaith eto, mae ein diolch i David Owen. Rydym yn hyderus y bydd y llyfr mor boblogaidd â chyfrolau cynt.

Mair and Terry Williams

Introduction

Some of the finest landscapes in South Wales can be found in the Rhondda Valleys, which run south from the mountains on the border of the Brecon Beacons National Park towards Cardiff, capital of Wales.

Right at the heart of the many towns and communities that make up Rhondda Fawr and Rhondda Fach are warm and friendly local people, known worldwide for their loyalty, capacity for hard work, and care for others.

But today we can easily pass by the relics and remains of the great mining industry that lead to the creation of our famous communities.

David Owen's book tells the story of village life and the pits of Rhondda – and as I spent many years working in the local mining industry I can vouch that his poignant account is informative and accurate.

This volume is a welcome reminder of men who worked deep underground and their families – the generations who helped to build a new society and economy here in Wales.

Cllr Islwyn Wilkins, Chairman, Rhondda Cynon Taf County Borough Council

Cyflwyniad

Mae peth o'r dirwedd fwyaf gogoneddus yn y Deheubarth i'w gweld yng nghylchoedd Cwm Rhondda wrth ichi deithio tua'r de o'r mynyddoedd sydd ar gyrion Parc Cenedlaethol Bannau Brycheiniog i gyfeiriad Caerdydd, ein Prifddinas.

Wrth galon yr amryw drefi a'r bröydd sy'n galon i Gwm Rhondda Fawr a Chwm Rhondda Fach, dewch chi ar draws pobl gyfeillgar a thwymgalon sy'n adnabyddus ar draws y byd am eu teyrngarwch, eu gallu i ymdopi â gwaith caled a'u gofal nhw dros eraill.

Erbyn heddiw, fodd bynnag, hawdd fyddai cerdded heibio i greiriau ac olion y diwydiant mwyngloddio anferth a arweiniodd at sefydlu'n cymunedau enwog ni yn y lle cyntaf.

Yn llyfr David Owen, cewch chi hanes bywyd pentrefol a glofeydd Cwm Rhondda - a gan i minnau dreulio blynyddoedd lawer yn gweithio yn y diwydiant mwyngloddio lleol, gallaf gadarnhau bod ei stori deimladwy yn un addysgol ac un sy'n sicr yn ei ffeithiau.

Mae'r gyfrol yma'n gyfie i'n hatgoffa ni am wŷr a weithiai dan ddaear ac am eu teuluoedd - y cenedlaethau hynny a fuodd yn gymorth i sefydlu cymdeithas ac economi newydd eu dydd yma yng Nghymru.

Y Cynghorydd Islwyn Wilkins, Cadeirydd, Cyngor Bwrdeistref Sirol Rhondda Cynon Taf

One
Trehafod, Llwyncelyn, Porth, Ynyshir

When people talk about the South Wales Coalfield they almost invariably think of 'The Rhondda Valley', the most intensively mined area in the world. The term 'Rhondda' applies to two valleys, so both 'Rhondda Valley' and the Welsh usage 'Cwm Rhondda' are somewhat misleading. There is the 'Big Rhondda', 'Y Rhondda Fawr', and the 'Little Rhondda', 'Y Rhondda Fach'. The Rhondda Fawr is fourteen miles long, extending from Pontypridd, where it joins the Vale of Taff, to Blaenrhondda at the northern end. The Rhondda Fach is seven miles long, from Porth at the junction with the Rhondda Fawr to Maerdy at the northern end. This volume provides an illustrated account of the development of the Rhondda Fach.

Back in the early years of the nineteenth century these were pleasant deep-set wooded vales, along which flowed rivulets so clear that the term 'Rhondda' is derived, according to some authorities, from two words meaning 'good water'. The syllable 'Rhon' is associated with the names 'Rhone' and 'Rhine', two of the major rivers of Europe, and 'da' is the Welsh word for good. However, by this time the 'good water' of Cwm Rhondda streams had been blackened for more than 100 years by the coal from more than fifty pits sunk, one every mile or so, along the base of the valleys. Around these pits grew the villages for the mineworkers, becoming townships, which eventually linked up their terraces in almost continuous succession along the valleys to provide housing for a population which at its maximum was 167,000.

In the late 1950s and early '60s nearly 13,000 men worked at thirteen collieries and produced approximately 2,900,000 tons a year, nearly one-seventh of the output of the South Wales Coalfield. This meant that 46,000 people, nearly half the population of the Rhondda, had a direct family association with the coal-mining industry. Many of the people of the Rhondda now work in factories outside the valleys or are engaged in work relating to the various activities of a busy community. All the factories depended on coal to supply them with fuel and power, either as coal in its prime form, as coke, or as electricity and gas obtained from coal. The people who ran the shops, the buses, the churches, the schools, the railways, the public houses, and the cinemas, also had a vital concern with the successful operation of the coal-mining industry, both in respect of its product and in the economic well-being of the town for the wages paid for winning that product.

Black gold – Aur Du. The Rhondda communities owe their existence to the coal-mining industry, though today the dependence on that industry has completely gone, as has the wealth that went with it, but Rhondda's fame lives on. Cwm Rhondda has been transformed from being the centre of heavy engineering and mining to being green and lush, and wildlife has reclaimed many of the areas, attracted by a cleaner river and regenerating environment.

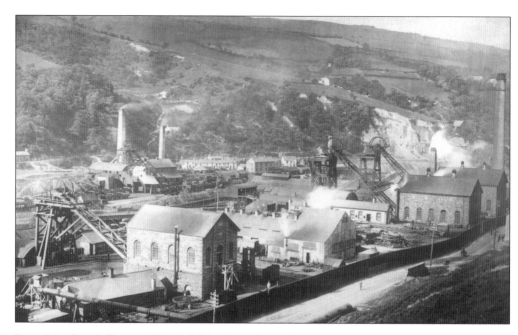

Lewis Merthyr Collieries, Trehafod (The English translation of Trehafod is: Tre(f) meaning town and Hafod meaning Summer Dwelling) in 1903. Left to right: Coed Cae, Hafod, Trefor and Bertie Pits. The Hafod concern was begun by two brothers, David and John Thomas. In 1850 they opened the Hafod Pit and although they reached the profitable Rhondda No. 3 and Hafod seams, the workings proved unfruitful and were abandoned. The second venture took place at Coed Cae in 1850 by Edward Mills, again the workings were abandoned due to water seepage.

Left: W.T. Lewis. In the mid-1870s, William Thomas Lewis, later Lord Merthyr, purchased the Hafod and Coed Cae shafts. The Coed Cae Pit was reopened in the early 1870s, but only the upper bituminous (Household) coal seam was worked. Lewis traded under the name of the Coed Cae Coal Co. until the pit closed in the 1930s. Hafod Pit is thought to have been worked from the 1880s; the bituminous seams were worked until 1893, after which date the deeper steam coal seams were worked by Powell Duffryn (PDs) known to many as the 'Poverty and Dole' group. *Right*: Author David Owen presenting Her Majesty Queen Elizabeth II his book *South Wales Collieries Volume Two* on her Golden Jubilee tour, 13 June 2002.

Lewis Merthyr Colliery canteen staff in 1952. The photograph includes Nestie, Iera Waite, Mrs Davies (manageress), Irene Sherry, Phyllis (cook), Mrs Lewis and Muriel Hippard. By the end of 1990 not one productive colliery existed in the Rhondda but the spirit of the turbulent and proud Rhondda past has been captured and preserved as an historic landmark at the Lewis Merthyr Colliery, now the Rhondda Heritage Park which was officially opened by Peter Walker Secretary of State on 11 September 1989.

Lewis Merthyr Colliery blacksmiths and strikers in 1937. The photograph includes Jack Owens, Reg Speed, Don Channing, Islwyn Thomas, Harold Rasmussen, Will Harries, Gwyn Bishop. By 1880 W.T. Lewis had sunk the Bertie shaft, and this was followed in 1890 by the Trefor shaft (Trefor and Bertie were named after W.T. Lewis' sons, and are still so named today at the Rhondda Heritage Park). By 1890 the colliery was known as the Lewis Merthyr Navigation Collieries Ltd, and from 1891 the five pits became the Lewis Merthyr Consolidated Collieries Ltd, employing some 5,000 men and producing almost a million tons of coal annually. On 22 November 1956 an explosion killed two men outright, with another seven dying later. The pit ceased winding coal in 1958 on its merger with Tŷ Mawr Colliery. Lewis Merthyr Colliery and Tŷ Mawr Colliery were both closed in 1983 by the National Coal Board (NCB).

Rhondda Valley Scouts, Beavers and Cubs fundraising for Tŷ Hafan Children's Hospice at the Rhondda Heritage Park Memorial in 2001. On 13 May 2000 actor Glyn Houston unveiled a memorial to the thousands of miners who died in the South Wales Collieries. The memorial is in the form of a 6ft-high miner's lamp, complete with an eternal flame.

Eirw Farm in the early years of the twentieth century. The Hafod community would have consisted of the Morgan family, who owned of the large Hafod Fawr estate, a number of smaller tenant farmers, craftsmen, a small group of labourers, servants, apprentices and shepherds. The community would have been self-sufficient, with their existence dependent on the traditional farming of sheep and some cattle.

Siloam Welsh Calvinistic Methodist chapel during the flood in 1938. The photograph includes Mr Rees the caretaker. Siloam chapel was built in 1849. With the growth of the new community came the growth of religion in Trehafod. The number of places of worship indicates the religious intensity of the village people. At chapels, Sunday schools were well attended as they acted as a form of education for the villagers' children.

Trehafod Road in 1906. People migrated into Trehafod primarily for coalmining purposes and it is no surprise that the 1851 census lists seventy-two coal miners, five labourers, three hauliers, three blacksmiths, two sinkers, one engineer and one coal agent. Other occupations that were listed include masons, farmers, farm labourers, a tailor, a horse follower and a railway policeman. Whilst the majority of women did not have occupations there were two dressmakers, two servants and a thirteen-year-old nurse.

WAF Margaret Kibble (*née* Jones – back row, second from left) in 1949.

Trehafod Blackpool outing in the 1950s. The photograph includes Cliff Jones, Jan Newman, Doreen Davies, Ierwen Newman, Mair Jones, Cyril Cannard, Jesse Newman, Cliff Martin, Bill Bowles, Mrs Jones, Olwen Newman, Bettie Williams, Meireon Newman, Tommy Ashford, Lynda Newman, Edith Powell and Vernon Bowkett.

Bryn Eirw church (Saint Barnabas) in 1905. Saint Barnabas, opened in 1892, is the only place of worship in Trehafod and is situated on the corner of Bryn Eirw. In 1887, a Sunday school was held in the surgery of Dr Naunton Davies, but was soon closed due to overcrowding. The Lewis Merthyr Colliery came to the rescue and placed the colliery reading room at the disposal of the church until 1892.

A view of Trehafod. The photograph was taken from the 'Tump' and was presented by Des Bird. Through the efforts of the congregation at Saint Barnabas £900 was raised to build a hall seating 250 people. This was built on the present site and was known as the Bryn Eirw Mission. After many more fundraising efforts the church acquired new pews and an organ. The church continued to flourish and in 1930 the name was changed to Saint Barnabas.

Hafod school. There were three schools: boys, girls and mixed infants, built in 1877. Much of the educational provision in Wales during the 1800s was through the astonishingly rich community life that existed in many areas. The choral festival, the Sunday school, the Eisteddfodau and the travelling schools. The Elementary Board Schools were set up under Forster's Act of Parliament in 1870. Under this Act local schools were established and these included Graig, Coedpenmaen, Hawthorn, Mill Street, Navigation, Porth, Treforest and Hafod.

Hafod Girls School standard 6b in 1931. Situated opposite the Vaughan's Arms, on Coed Cae Road, the master was Mr John Evans, the mistress was Elizabeth Thomas and the infants' teacher was Mary Evans. With the expansion of the local colliery and an increase in pupil numbers, the school was resited in Wayne Street and has remained there ever since.

Hafod school in 1936. The photograph includes Dennis Hunkin, George Downes, Dennis Grant, Valmai Venting, Joyce Hicks, Billy Mauley, Frankie Minty, Ken Watkins, Kenneth Davies, John Martin, Eirfryn Newman and Ken Willcocks. In the 1960s it became a primary school and retains the name of Hafod school. Unfortunately this picture has been damaged, but its rarity justifies its inclusion here.

Hafod schoolchildren with Rhondda Cynon Taf Council Leader Pauline Jarman AM at the opening of the all-new children's Energy Zone at the Rhondda Heritage Park on Friday 24 May 2002. Like the population of Trehafod, the number of pupils has varied considerably. Probably the greatest number was 900, recorded in the 1940s, the reason for this being the large number of evacuees that came into the area attending the school.

Llwyncelyn (Hollybush) Colliery in 1900; height above ordnance datum 290 feet. The Colliery was sunk in 1851 by David James to the Rhondda No. 2 and the Rhondda No. 3 seams. The next owners were T. Edmunds and then the Lewis Merthyr Consolidated Collieries Limited in 1891. On 1 December 1853 the accident reports show that nineteen-year-old haulier S.W. James Rees was killed by an explosion. Llwyncelyn Colliery closed in 1895.

One memorable and leading mining figure to emerge out of the harsh political strife of Cwm Rhondda was Arthur James Cook (1884-1931), who resided at 52 Nyth Brân (Crows Nest) Terrace, Llwyncelyn. He started work as a labourer in the Trefor Pit and soon worked his way to becoming a haulier. Cook's political career was soon underway and he became a delegate to the Lewis Merthyr Employees Joint Committee while working at Coed Cae Pit. His political views were responsive to socialism and he became deeply involved in the South Wales Miners Federation in 1911. A.J. Cook later became the General Secretary of the British Miners and led them during the struggles and hardship of the General Strike in 1926. He led the miners by example, surrendering his union salary, living only on lockout pay and living on trains as he shuttled from coalfield to coalfield, preaching his revolutionary socialism to crowds of up to 100,000. Prime Minister Stanley Baldwin called it 'Cook's Strike'. Cartoons in the national press pilloried A.J. Cook, and the Cabinet considered ordering his arrest because of the powerful influence he exerted on the working classes. Arthur James Cook led the fight for justice for the men of an industry in which a man died every six hours and another was badly injured every two minutes.

Twenty-two-year-old Arthur Morris of Gethin Terrace, Llwyncelyn. Arthur worked at Lewis Merthyr and Tŷ Mawr Collieries for thirty years and later became foreman in the washery.

A view of Llwyncelyn (beyond Lewis Merthyr Colliery in the photograph) in 1905.

The barn of Nyth Brân (Crows Nest) House. Gruffydd Morgan (Guto Nyth Brân), who resided at Nyth Brân House, was a shepherd on the local hills surrounding the farm and the legend goes that his speed and endurance were developed by the daily rounding up of sheep to make him one of the fastest runners ever known.

Nyth Brân House with eighty-five-year-old Betty Vaughn in 2002. This, the present day Nyth Brân House, was built in 1912 and is locally known as the 'White House'. On Guto's tombstone (Guto died in 1737) at the parish church of Llanwynno, it is recorded that he covered twelve miles of mountain ground in seven minutes less than an hour!

Saint Luke's Church Ladies Guild in 1951. The photograph includes Mrs Rees, Lottie Phillips, Little Mari, Muriel Hippard, Ray Hitchcombe, Hetty Morgan, Mrs Backley, Mrs Garwood, Mrs Jones and Mrs Davies. Saint Luke's church began as a corrugated-steel building in 1907, and the present-day Saint Luke's was built in 1909. The vicars from 1907 were William Thomas, 1907-13; Daniel Mark, 1914-28; Tom Jones, 1928-37; Jeffrey Jones, 1937-58; Martin Bowen, 1959-67; Denis Butler, 1967-79; Philip Morris, 1980-88; Peter Leonard, 1988-94; Graham Lloyd 1996- current at time of writing (2002).

Saint Luke's Church Choir on the Coronation of Queen Elizabeth II, 2 June 1953. The photograph includes: Ron Ninnis, Keith Davies, Lennard George Hippard, Alun Rees, Peter Vaughan, Allen Hippard, Martin Vaughn. The curates from 1908 were R.G. Martin, 1908-10; Joseph Jones, 1910-12; D.M. Griffiths, 1913-14; J. Parsons, 1914-15; W. Thomas, 1915-17; D.T. Jones, 1917-26; T. Leyshon, 1927-33; Brynmor Davies, 1934-36; Ivor Jones, 1936-37; Norman Griffiths, 1937-42; John Dale, 1942-48; S.L. Owen, 1948-49; W.T. Price, 1950-56; R.S. Richardson, 1960-62; Glyn Derek Price, 1976-81. Margaret Maund was the last curate in 1994.

Football match, Llwyncelyn men versus Llwyncelyn ladies on the 'Rats' (fire station) in 1926. The men played with their hands tied behind their backs.

Llwyncelyn Welfare football team on the 'Rats'. Sport was a rebuff to the workaday world. Rhondda embraced it wholeheartedly from that day to this. Maybe it was underground toil that created with such frequency the muscular rugby forwards who caused the name 'Rhondda Forwards' to be applied to all the hard men of the pack. In 1844, Lewis Edwards developed the Nyth Brân Level. In 1963, caravans were made available for fifty colliery workers at Llwyncelyn Welfare Ground.

Harlequins RUFC training at Llwyncelyn Welfare Ground in 2002. Left to right, back row: Scott Holland, James Evans, Scott Vynor, Mark Pritchard, Gerwyn Harris, Mathew Adams, Ossian Griffiths, Mark Evans, Gerald Morgan. Front row: Mark Parry, Justin Townsend, Christian Trivet, Adrian John, Craig John, Andrew Williams, Jason Gillard, Gareth Barkers, Owen Jones, Jason Jones, Christian Rees, Sean Davies.

Washing the flagstone pavement outside the front door in the 1930s. Slate and pennant sandstone still predominate in a self-improving Rhondda where red and green roof tiles and colour-wash walls stand out as daubs of newness. Larger houses are quite distinct amidst the ranks of terraces. The number of shops that grew in the villages of Cwm Rhondda evidently proved the self-sufficiency of the people in a rapidly expanding industrial area.

Llwyncelyn Bridge in 1934 with the 'Rats' on the left in the photograph. In 1920 the shops in Llwyncelyn were: Richard Hall, hairdresser, 45 Nyth Brân Terrace; George Hillier, 44 Nyth Brân Terrace; David Jenkins, 46 Nyth Brân Terrace; Thomas Lewis, boot repairer, 42 Nyth Brân Terrace; Margaret Morgan, 67 Lesley Terrace; Evan James Morris, 21 Gethin Terrace; Hugh Thomas, 37 Gethin Terrace; Jas Thomas, grocer, 43 Nyth Brân Terrace. Catherine Williams of 27 Gethin Terrace was the midwife and Elizabeth Mary Williams was the landlady of the Llwncelyn Hotel.

Gethin Terrace residents celebrating the marriage of HRH Prince Charles in 1981. From left to right: T. Clapworthy, B. Price, E. Jones, G. Vaughan and his faithful companion Henry; D. Jones, I. Rees, A. Morris.

Llwyncelyn residents celebrating the Queen's Golden Jubilee, 10 June 2002. The photograph includes Lena, Ellis, Jessica, Carry, Lindsey, Sarah, Haley, Joshua, Jodie, Daniel, Jodie Williams, Elise, Victoria, Shauna, Katherine, Ryan, Lucy, Rhys, Carla, Calum, Hannah, Emily, Chloe, Danielle and Josh.

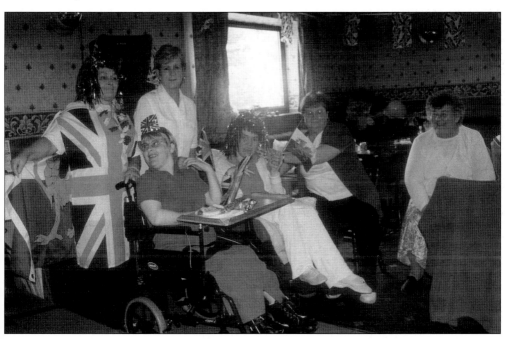

Llwyncelyn residents celebrating the Queen's Golden Jubilee, 10 June 2002. The photograph includes Pat Williams, Marlene Graham, Pam Jones, Lee Rossiter, Caroline Jones and Gaynor England.

Llwyncelyn schools in 2002. The Welsh school is on the left and the English school is on the right in the photograph.

Llwyncelyn junior school in 1912. Llwyncelyn school opened in 1904. The photograph includes Doris Audrey and Frances Salter, formerly of 56 Lewis Terrace.

Llwyncelyn infant school in 1934. The photograph includes Gracie Griffiths, Nancy Harding, May Williams, Maldwyn Griffiths, Mervyne Davies, David Morris, Phillip Morris, Islwyn Rhydderch, Cyril Whitenham, Ivor Lynham, Dillwyn Durbin, Iuaun Gwynne, Ritchie Rowley, Gwyn Harries, Dennis Cooke, Sammy Day, Cliff Roberts, Gracie Griffiths, Mona Harding, Ethel Stranks, Jackie Bean and Gladys Evans.

Llwyncelyn school, Saint David's Day, 1 March 1955. The photograph includes teachers Mr Reynolds, Miss Harris and Mr Smith and pupils Pam Lewis, Allan Rees, Ann Chapman, Diane Ford, Brenda Paine, Mair Williams. After passing their examinations during the depression of the 1930s the school leavers had to seek work in the cities and towns of England, leaving only the young and the old behind. Many of their fathers were out of work and on the dole.

Tynewydd Colliery, Porth (Gateway), in 1890. The colliery was sunk in 1852 at a depth of 270 feet by the Troedyrhiw Coal Company. At approximately 4.00 p.m. on Wednesday 11 April 1877 the Tynewydd Colliery was inundated with water from the old workings of the adjoining Hinde's Upper Cymmer Colliery. At the time of the inundation there were fourteen men in the pit, of whom four were unfortunately drowned and one killed by compressed air, leaving nine men imprisoned by the water. Of this number, four were released after eighteen hours imprisonment and five after nine days imprisonment. It was in effecting the release of these latter five that those distinguished services were rendered which the conferring of the 'Albert Medal of the First Class' is intended to recognize. Until the Tynewydd Colliery disaster the Albert Medal First and Second Class had been given only for bravery in saving life at sea. Then came Queen Victoria's announcement:

> The Albert Medal, hitherto only bestowed for gallantry in saving life at sea, shall be extended to similar actions on land and that the first medals struck for this purpose shall be conferred on the heroic rescuers of the Welsh Miners.

The *London Gazette* published the list on 7 August 1877 as follows:

> The Queen has been graciously pleased to confer the 'Albert Medal of the First Class' on: Daniel Thomas Colliery Proprietor Brithwynydd Rhondda Valley, William Beith Mechanical Engineer of Harris Navigation Colliery, Quakers Yard, Isaac Pride Collier Llwyncelyn Colliery, Rhondda, John William Howell Collier Ynyshir Colliery, Rhondda. The Queen has been graciously pleased to confer the 'Albert Medal of the Second Class' on: George Albert Collier Tynewydd Colliery, Rhondda, Charles Baynham Collier Brithwynydd Colliery, Rhondda, Richard Hopkins Collier Ynyshir Colliery, Rhondda, Richard Howells Overman Tynewydd Colliery, Rhondda, Charles Oatridge Collier Tynewydd Colliery, Rhondda, John Williams Collier Pontypridd Colliery, Edward David Collier Hafod Colliery, Rhondda, William Morgan Hafod Colliery, Rhondda, David Rees Fireman Tynewydd Colliery, Rhondda, Rees Thomas Collier Tynewydd Colliery, Rhondda.

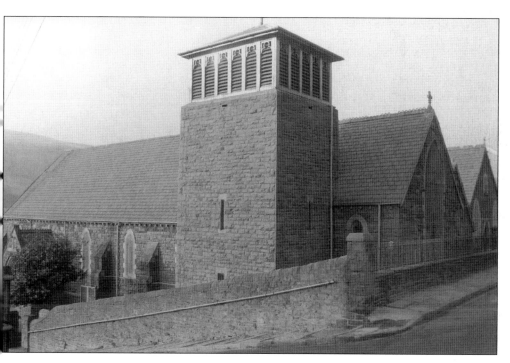

Saint Paul's church, Porth, in 1990. Saint Paul's church was erected in 1886 at a cost of £1,500. It is an edifice of stone, in the early English style, consisting of chancel, nave and a turret containing one bell. In 1896 a new organ was installed at a cost of £250. The church was enlarged in 1910 with a seating capacity of 530.

Interior of Saint Paul's church, Porth, in 1910. Charabanc trips and Sunday school outings, beginning in the vestries of churches and chapels, punctuated a life of work, transporting Rhondda people away to happy, noisy, bustling Barry Island or Porthcawl.

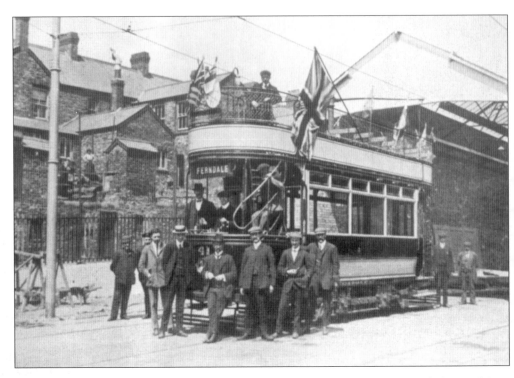

A tram at Porth depot gaily decorated for the visit of King George V and Queen Mary, Thursday 27 June 1912. On 1 February 1934, the last tram ran in the Rhondda and as it returned to the depot at the end of the day, a huge crowd sang 'Farewell My Own True Love'.

The machine shop at Porth depot 7 July 1955. Road and railway transport serving the valleys present many features of great historical interest. Following the opening to Dinas in 1841, the railway was next extended in 1849, northward along the Rhondda Fach from Porth to Ynyshir for mineral traffic only. In 1856 this branch was extended from Ynyshir to Ferndale and in 1886 the lines in this valley were completed by extending ownership from Ferndale to Maerdy. The railway from Ferndale to Maerdy was opened and owned privately by Mordecai Jones in 1877.

Tynewydd Square, Porth, in 1934.

A view of Porth from Cymmer in 1912.

Porth Square in 1880.

Porth Square in 1900.

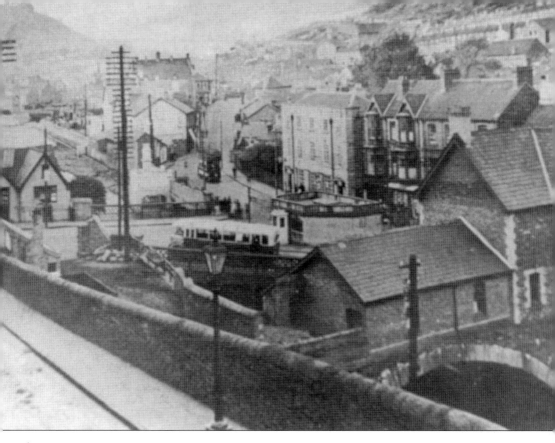

Porth Square in 1933.

Porth Square in the new Millennium.

Porth Carnival in 1910.

Rhondda Urban District Steam Refuse Lorry (Ash Lorry) at Porth in 1922.

Baden Powel Club outing to Porthcawl in 1951.

Porth YMCA in 1964. The photograph includes Ken Owen, Clive Williams, Alan Pearce, Ray Rees (Welsh judo lightweight champion) and Roy Corish.

Porth County school (PCCS Gwell Dysgna Golud) in 1905. The foundation stone reads: 'This plot of ground consisting of 10,000 sq yds was given free by the Turbervills of Ewenny Priory and this memorial stone was laid by Mrs L.E. Picton Turbervill on the 5 February 1894'. The boys school opened 23 September 1896 and the girls school opened in 1913.

Porth Higher Elementary (Grammar) School rugby team in the 1935/36 season. From left to right, back row: J. Harris, W. Jones, H. Davies, E. Morgan, J. Vaughan. Third row: G. Howell, G. Lewis, K. Davies, E. Owen, R. James, S. Bucknell, Mr P.S. Kingdon BSc (teacher). Second row: Mr G. Davies BA (headteacher), G. Davies, N. Jones, I. Lewis (captain), H. Edwards, L.R. Lewis, Mr W. Morris (sports teacher). Front row: G. Jones, I. Griffiths.

Porth Higher Elementary (Grammar) School hockey team in the 1948/49 season. From left to right, back row: B. Stacey, A. Edwards, B. Thomas, Y. McLeish, R. Copleston, S. Trowbridge, I. Jarman. Front row: Miss I. Thomas (sports teacher), G. Owen, J. Lindsay, P. Roberts (captain), J. Michael, G. Barnett, Mr I. Howells BA (headteacher). Porth Higher Elementary (Grammar) School opened in 1900.

Porth Higher Elementary (Grammar, Technical) School staff in 1968. The photograph includes Ieuan Thomas, John Venables, Terry Williams, Charles Griffith, Ieuan Parry, Roy Keaton, Emrys James, Hubert Volk, Desmond Harris, Derwent Jones, Theo Jones, Elfed Bowen, Glyn Richards, Ann Lindsey, Shirley Anstiss, Olwen Ladd, Emlyn Morgan (headteacher), Olive Evans, Evelyn Morris, Marie Jones and Pat Luther.

The Lady Lewis Colliery, Ynyshir (Long Island or Meadow) in 1906. The colliery was opened in 1904 by Lewis Merthyr Consolidated Collieries Limited. Height above ordnance datum, 361ft 6in. Rhondda No. 2 seam at 149ft 5in; Rhondda No. 3 at 362ft 6in; Hafod at 525ft 3in; Lower Four-Feet at 1,070ft 7in; Six-Feet at 1,133ft; Upper Six-Feet at 1,214ft 11in; Lower Nine-Feet at 1,278ft 2in; Bute at 1,287ft 1in; Fault; Yard at 1,294ft 6in; Upper and Middle Seven-Feet seam at 1,307ft 10in; Five-Feet at 1,404ft; and Gellideg at 1,426ft 6in.

The Lady Lewis Colliery, Ynyshir officials' outing in the 1930s. The colliery was owned by the Powell Duffryn Steam Coal Company prior to nationalization in 1947. Lady Lewis Colliery was closed in 1950 by the National Coal Board.

Lower end of Ynyshir, 1900, with the Ynyshir Colliery on the left. Ynyshir Colliery, locally known as Jones's Pit, was sunk by Messrs Shepherd and Evans in 1849 and seven years later it was purchased by Francis Crawshay to supply coal for his tinplate works at Treforest, the colliery employing about 100 men. In 1873 the colliery was owned by Thomas Jones of Maerdy House, Ynyshir. The shaft was 198ft deep and the colliery worked the Rhondda No. 2 seam at a section of 2ft 6in to 3 feet, supplying their own coking ovens. On Saturday 12 May 1877 there was an explosion in the Ynyshir Steam Coal Colliery owned by Daniel and James Thomas. At midday three men John Howell, John Hopkins and Abraham Dodds were driving a windway between the two shafts. They were drilling ahead and had holed into the passageway on the other side. Gas came through the holes made by the drills and burned in their Davy lamps. The lamps became hotter and hotter and Dodd suggested it was time to put them out. Hopkins assured him that there was no danger as he had been in the other passageway and it did not contain a dangerous quantity of gas. When the hole had been enlarged, Dodd put his head and arms through. At that moment there was a lurid flash and the explosion hurled Dodd back many yards. He suffered serious burns and experienced a great deal of pain. Abraham Dodd was a man who with Isaac Pride took part in the final, most dangerous part of the rescue at Tynewydd Colliery and if any man deserved to be recognised for his bravery that man was Dodd. Why does his name not appear? One can only guess at the explanation. Perhaps someone who reads these words may be in a position to clear the matter finally. It would give pleasure to another generation of Rhondda people to honour a man whose deeds were no less than those who were honoured by the Queen. The Forest Fach coal seam was at a depth of 149ft 11in with a thickness of 10in and the Rhondda No. 2 seam at a depth of 174ft with a thickness of 2ft 10in. Ynyshir Colliery closed in 1909.

General view of Ynyshir, 1910, with the Standard Colliery in the background. The Standard Colliery was sunk by James 'Siamps' Thomas in 1876, and by 1878 was producing 188,366 tons of coal per year. The Rhondda No. 2 coal seam was found at a depth of 229ft 11in. In 1914 the Standard Colliery amalgamated with the United National Collieries Company Limited, who employed over 1,300 people and produced over 36,000 tons of coal and later became part of the Ocean Coal Company. The colliery was acquired by the National Coal Board in 1947 and kept open for ventilation and pumping mine water only.

Bryn Awel, former home of James 'Siamps' Thomas, born in Bedwellty in 1817, became an underground doorboy at the age of six. He also became a fireman, an overman and a colliery manager. Bryn Awel, situated opposite the former colliery site, is now a nursing home for the elderly.

Saron chapel in 1906. In 1884 the English Baptist cause was started by Mr and Mrs David John of No. 1 Weston Terrace. David John was said to have been the pioneer of the movement and the leader of a small band of people. Their vision was to have a chapel of their own and this dream was achieved when the Welsh Congregationalists outgrew their chapel at Ynshir Road in 1885 and built Saron chapel.

Saint Anne's church in 1930. In 1888 Ynyshir was formed into an ecclesiastical parish out of Llanwynno and Ystradyfodwg. It is now called Rhondda Cynon Taf and is in the rural deanery of Rhondda and archdeaconry and diocese of Llandaff. The church of Saint Anne is a building of stone, consisting of chancel nave aisles, north porch and a belfry containing two bells. It has a seating capacity of 550. There are two stained-glass windows in the church dedicated to the memory of Thomas Jones esq. and his daughter. A brass eagle lectern was presented in 1908 by Sir William James Thomas and his sisters in memory of their father.

Ynyshir Albions in the 1909/10 season.

Ynyshir Road in the 1920s.

Mr Barnett, greengrocer and florist, Ynyshir, in the 1930s.

The Co-operative Society delivery cart, Ynyshir, in the 1930s.

Ynyshir and Wattstown fife and drum band in the 1920s.

Left: Weston Terrace celebrating His Majesty King George VI's Coronation in 1937. *Right*: Mrs Mary-Ellen Bloomfield and her daughter Laura at Weston Terrace celebrating the Coronation.

Left: Four generations. Garfield Bloomfield (front right), daughter Eira (back left), grand-daughter Joyce (back right), great grandson Keith (front left) in 1963. *Right*: South Street residents celebrating the investiture of HRH Prince Charles in July 1969.

British harmonica tape champion and first Dave Jackson Rose Bowl winner Ray Rees of Graig Terrace, Ynyshir, in 1983. Left to right: Mrs Jackson, Frank Eatwell, Ray Rees. Ray was British tape champion for the years 1983, 1985, 1986, 1987, 1995 and 1996.

Ynyshir Boys School in the 1920s. Ynyshir Boys School log books begin in 1881. Much of the educational provision in Wales during the 1800s was through the astonishingly rich community life that existed in many areas, including the choral festival, the Sunday school, the Eisteddfodau and the travelling schools.

Ynyshir Junior School standard 5a, the eleven-plus scholarship class in 1956. Left to right, back row: M. Miles, D. Llewellyn, P. Bents, J. Isaacs, M. Hopkins, S. Burden, C. Jones, E. Cotter, L. Dowler, M. Howells. Third row: Mr T. Walters (teacher), M. Atkins, N. Spencer, J. Mathews, L. Foxwell, S. Davies, T. Godfrey, B. Evans, R. James, Mr C. Evans (headteacher). Second row: R. Jones, D. Owen, J. Palmer, S. Roberts, R. Giddings, B. Jenkins, T. Miles, R. Edwards, K. Ivins, N. Venables. Front row: M. Stephens, L. Price, J. Roberts, W. John, G. ?, R. Jones.

Ynyshir school summer play scheme, 22 July 2002. The photograph includes Kayley, Deva, Laura, Kelly, Emily, Jodie, Heather, Catharine, Tom, Natalie, Hazel, Christine, Sadie, Lloyd. Activities include: Painting, candle making, jewellery making, ball games, pool and outings to the coast and cinema.

Ynyshir school summer play scheme, 22 July 2002. The photograph includes T. Rook, G. Jones, T. Lewis, E. Edwards, P. Weston, L. Price, T. Bird, S. Fowler, T. Fowler, S. Lewis, R. Lewis, J. Gower, L. Jones, A. Jones, M. Lewis, R. Lewis, D. Edwards, J. Weston, H. Weston, S.L. Price, J. Price, K. Bird, L. Bird, S. Fowler, A. Fowler.

How Green Was My Valley

In the early days of Cwm Rhondda
When the mountains were woodland green,
The air was filled with songbirds singing,
The rivers ran fresh and clean.
Then came Walter Coffin
To sink his Dinas mine,
It was the start of a new era,
The start of a different time.
The hills were stripped of their woodlands
Cwm Rhondda Rivers all turned black,
The days of farming and beauty were never coming back.
Now the mines have finished,
Their black tips remind us still
It was they that took the beauty
From our wooded hills.

Dennis Morris, retired mining deputy

Cwm Rhondda Christmas Eve Memories

It was Christmas Eve and Mam had just undressed me ready for bed. I stood shivering and barefoot on the cold linoleum clad in my long, winceyette nightdress in the unheated front bedroom of our terraced house, with the flickering light of the candle throwing mysterious and weird shadows on the wall.

As Mam was busily putting clothes into the big chest of drawers, I ran to the window, which was misted over, rubbed my hand over the icy pane and looked out towards the Gwyngul Mountain.

Darkness had descended like a black, velvet cloak over Cwm Rhondda; the night sky was a deep blue and a pale, yellow rubber-ball moon floated along.

It was a clear, frosty night and stars winked in the distance. Suddenly, as I watched, a fluffy cloud like a gigantic ice-cream cone appeared silhouetted against the dark blue of the sky floating above Old Smokey, the black pyramid-shaped Tylorstown coal tip. As the cloud rose higher and higher its shape changed – it looked like a sleigh being drawn by reindeer.

Excitedly, I called out to Mam. She looked through the window and said it was, without doubt, Siôn Corn's (Father Christmas's) sleigh and that he was on his way from Greenland to our house and that I'd better jump into bed quickly or he wouldn't be paying us a visit.

Hawys Glyn James

Two
Wattstown, Pontygwaith, Stanleytown, Penrhys

In the late 1870s two shafts were sunk at Pont-Y-Cwtch, later to be known as Wattstown. In 1880 the pit was owned by the National Steam Coal Company and Henry Lewis was the manager. The colliery was locally known as Cwtch, and was sunk to the Six-Feet seam at a depth of 454 yards. The downcast shaft was 17ft 6in in diameter and the upcast shaft 14ft in diameter. In 1900 the colliery employed 1,118 men. The first major explosion was on Friday 18 February 1887 and was caused by shotfiring. It claimed the lives of thirty-nine men and boys. The second explosion was on Tuesday 11 July 1905 and killed 119 men and boys. This explosion was also caused by shotfiring. National Colliery was closed on 22 November 1968 by the National Coal Board.

Pont-Y-Gwaith translates as 'Bridge of Work'. The village can be said to be a typical Welsh mining settlement of some 600 dwellings, dating from the early 1900s. Ironstone was being mined in Hirwaun – at the heads of the valleys – as early as 1575. Anthony Morley, a Sussex ironmaster, brought the environment of industry to Llanwynno and Merthyr Tydfil. There is possibly a strong connection between the name of Pontygwaith and Furnace Road, as one of Morley's furnaces was situated on the spot where the mountainside houses begin (Tylorstown End). There was also a forge nearby. Furnace Road of course was the old Parish Road to Llanwynno, the river being the boundary between the ancient parishes of Llanwynno and Ystradyfodwg.

Stanleytown, on the eastern side of the valley, and once a walk for the Cistercian monks, enjoys longer periods of sunshine and higher temperatures. The west side of the valleys are often in the shadow of the mountains behind them, particularly in winter when even the midday sun is low in the sky. No collieries exist in Cwm Rhondda today, but the area bears striking evidence of the coal-mining industry. All around we see mighty tips of spoil, though now mostly grass-covered. Sites of 'pit heads' with winding gear, drams and coal wagons etc. have disappeared. Coal mining here came and went within 100 years.

Penrhys has been in turn famous, forgotten and notorious. For 400 years, from the early Middle Ages until the Reformation, the Ancient Celtic well and the Medieval Marian Shrine were amongst the most famous sites of pilgrimage throughout Southern Britain. Mair o Benrhys was celebrated in poem and in song. Standing where the roads of prehistoric people met, the great ridge roads were joined by a track on the saddle across Penrhys. It served to connect these roads and the river fords across the two Rhondda rivers. Just below the Penrhys ridge is a well, which dates from pre-history and was Christianized by Celtic monks. Thousands of pilgrims come to receive the water from the ancient well (reputed to have miraculous healing powers) and to pray at the statue on the brow of the hill.

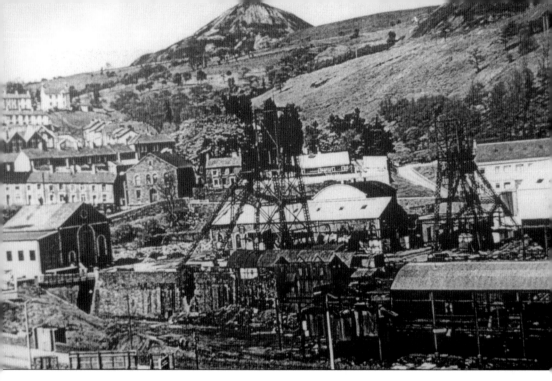

National Colliery, Wattstown in 1970. Height above ordnance datum 453 feet. In the late 1870s two shafts were sunk at Pont-Y-Cwtch, later to be known as Wattstown (named after Edmund Hannay Watts).

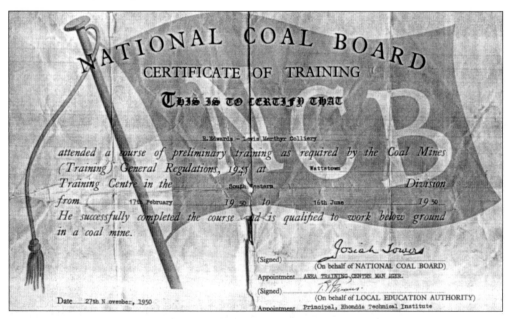

National Coal Board Certificate of Training, dated 27 November 1950. The certificate reads: 'This is to certify that R. Edwards attended a course of preliminary training as required by the Coal Mines (training) General Regulations, 1945 at Wattstown Training Centre in the south western division from 17 February 1950 to 16 June 1950. He successfully completed the course and is qualified to work below ground in a coal mine.'

National Colliery, Wattstown Lodge Banner in 1959. The photograph includes Dai 'Sarge' Thomas, Len Jones, Jack Lloyd, Tom Celely, Alf King, Ned 'Hangman' Jones, Alby Huzzle, Bunny, W.J. Thomas, Eddie Peel, Idris Griffiths, Billy Woods, J. Jones, Mog Thomas, Ivor Rowlands and Alwyn Evans.

Saint Thomas's church, Wattstown, in 1990. Wattstown, once a hamlet, is situated one and a half miles south of Tylors Town (Tylorstown). Saint Thomas's Mission church was attached to Saint Ann's church at Ynyshir, was an iron structure; the Revd Pierce Price was curate in 1920.

Wattstown Carnival in 1912. An extract from the reverse side of the postcard reads: 'Dear Gwen. I am sending you part of our Carnival, you will see many faces you know, see Tom Thomas in front opposite Charlie Isaac on his bike, see his sister behind as a darkey, that girl Griffiths. Bryn Isaac with his bike took first prize, he and his bike was dressed all in coloured paper. Lalla Gally behind took first prize for fancy dress little boy blue she looked a treat in blue tights, Mr Rees the Attendance Officer took the photos. Dai went to Blackpool last night, Cassie Hicks got a baby girl. I am sending you a paper for you to know who had prizes and some other news about Watts Town. Love from all, mother.'

Wattstown in 1950.

Wattstown in 1950. In 1920 Joseph Thomas was the landlord and the shops in Wattstown were: Canadian Meat Supply Co. (butchers), George Davies, John Davies (fried fish dealer), William Day (newsagent), William Evans, Annie Heycock (butcher), Mary Jones (draper), Sarah Anne Jones (draper), Irene Meredith, Thomas Powel (grocer), Evan Rees (boot repairer), Ebenezer Reynolds (butcher), Robert Sampson (newsagent), Tabitha Saunders, Mary Stroud (baker), Thomas & Evans (grocers), Charles Thomas (dairyman), Richard Thomas, William John Wells (fried fish dealer) Thomas Willcocks (boot maker) William Williams & Co. (grocers), George Morris Hill (landlord) Wattstown Hotel (Tommy John's).

Left: In the centre is Ritchie Marden, 1st Battalion Welch Regiment in 1947 holding a grenade. *Right*: Alan 'Buzz' Atkins, Mal Palmer 1st Battalion, Welch Regiment, on HMS *Fearless* in 1967.

Wattstown RFC in the early 1970s. The photograph includes: Dai Jones, Paul Horton, Terry Jarvis, John Harris, 'Jebbie' Lee, Mile Coleman, Stuart Marden, Ron James, Steven Thomas.

Wattstown Under-10 Mini Rugby Team 1994/95 season. Left to right, back row: M. Davies, S. Thomas, C. Jones, S. Phillips, G. Haynes, M. Evans, S. Weston, S. Roberts, D. Roberts, D. Auger. Front row: K. Salter, J. Jones, S. Phelps, Sam Jenkins (sponsor), W. Facey, M. Evans, D. England.

Wattstown residents celebrating the Queen's Golden Jubilee, 10 June 2002. The photograph includes Lynda Maize, Martin Maize, Stephan Marden, Eunice Langford, Mair Llewellyn, Dai Morris, Muriel Semmons, Sheryl Morris, Ray Llewellyn, Ray England, Joyce Evans, Betty Morgan, Ann Hopkins, Russell Palmer, Joyce Evans, Thomas Stewart, Mike Bounds, Kalem Semmons, Louise Morris, Catherine Gibbs.

Sunbeam Owners Club on tour. The photograph includes Dai Lye and Terry Palmer, with Mal Palmer leading the bikers on his Triumph Tiger 90, 350cc twin engine, which he bought from Phil Jones of Ystrad, Rhondda, in 1962.

Aberllechau Junior School's cup-winning football team of the 1956/57 season. Left to right, back row: Mr Roberts (teacher), Mr Owens (teacher). Middle row: Roy Evans, Ken Jones, Colin Day, David Howells, Robert Day, Bryn Roberts. Front row: Spencer Wiltshire, David Allen, Ray Hughes, Colin Diamond, Mike Davies, Mal Palmer, Haydn Howells. Aberllechau Junior School opened in 1887.

Aberllechau Junior School in 1957. Left to right, back row: Miss Davies (teacher), Derrick Evans, Colin Harvey, Clive Francis, Glyn Thomas, Wayne Warner. Third row: Angela Gerry, Paul Turton, Sheryl Williams, Corrine Mathews, Marilyn Lloyd, Wendy Thomas, June Studley, Cilla Bowen, Barbara Ellis, Jimmy Williams. Second row: Jean Davies, Marilyn Jones, Sheryl Morgan, Aureole King, Janice Jenkins, Eleanor Huzzle. Front row: Denzel Lee, Hugh Rhydderch, Richard Davies, Terry Davies, Terry Palmer.

Aberllechau Happy Tots Playgroup, Saint David's Day, 1 March 2000. Left to right, back row: David Easley, Iwan Davies, Kieron Assiratti, Craig Haynes, Sam Harding. Front row: Jordan Waite, Daisy ?, Kelsey Hancock, Ffion Jenkins, Jarred Hammond, Georgeia Evans. When you are over two years old this is the place to start your pre-school days.

Aberllechau Happy Tots Playgroup, 2 July 2002. The photograph includes Julie Jenkins, Jackie Winterburn, Chloe Jones, Dafydd Owen, Levi Evans, Connor Slee, Molly Philpot, Ellie Perkins, Kirshia Jonen. The main hall is splendidly decorated and it has a warm and welcoming feel for all young new pre-school starters.

The opening of Saint Mary Magdalene church, Pontygwaith. The photograph includes Mr Walters (station master), Mr Seldon, Mr Charles Evans, Mrs Walters, May Walters, Mr Davies (draper), Mrs Evans. Saint Mary Magdalene church celebrated its centenary in 1996. It was consecrated on 6 July 1896, having been built to the design of a Mr Halliday on a site which was part of the farm of Penrhys Isaf, which itself was the property of the Llewellyn family of Baglan Hall. It cost £3,348 to build.

The church organ in Saint Mary Magdalene church in 2000. There are two other Llewellyn churches in the Rhondda and a visit to Saint George's, Cwmparc, and Saint Peters, Pentre, will show many similarities in design. The vicars of Saint Mary Magdalene church were: 1900 J. Rees, 1914 J. Humphreys, 1924 H. Withers, 1934 T.J. Goodwin, 1942 J.L. White, 1947 I.B. Jones, 1953 J.J. Davies, 1961 J.H. Cox, 1986 E. Hastey, 1988 A.E. Morton, 1994 R.O.L. Lowndes. Saint Mary Magdalene church closed on 8 November 1997.

A Sketch of Soar chapel. It may seem strange to us now, that the founding of a chapel should be in a pub. It was in the long room of the Bridgend Inn that sixty-eight men and women met on 9 December 1895. Of that number some forty-five had brought letters from Ebenezer, Tylorstown to start a new Independent chapel in Pontygwaith. Within a few years they had built a small vestry on the west side of the main road, Llewellyn Street. In the first nine years they called and lost two ministers, but by 1905 they were able to make two major decisions, the first to call Parch Joseph Evans to minister to them and the second to build a large chapel on the same site as the vestry. The chapel was opened in 1907. Within a short time the building showed the cracks and fissures of subsidence and it was condemned by the authorities in 1916. They searched for and found a solid foundation for their new meeting place on land on the banks of the river near Madalene Street. Soar was opened in 1924 and though it has had a facelift it remains essentially the same today.

1895 - 1995

Llewellyn Street, Pontygwaith, 11 July 1908. One of the nicest features of the town now is Grove House Court, the private housing development built on the former brewery site. Pontygwaith has two streets where there are no houses, David Street and Pontygwaith Road. David Street is the one leading to Madeline Street from Llewellyn Street and Pontygwaith Road is the one from Station Road to Furnace Road.

Llewellyn Street, Pontygwaith in 1930. In 1895 the shops in Pontygwaith were: D. Ashton & Co (grocers and provisions), David Bowen (clothier), Daniel Davies (grocer), James Davies, Stephen Davies (boot dealer), Thos Davies (greengrocer), William Davies (china dealer), Edwards & Sons (dairyman), David Evans, Evan Evans (draper), John Harris (butcher), Evan Hughes (greengrocer), W. Jenkins, Jones & Co (drapers and post office), J.E. Jones (grocers, provision and builders), J.R. Jones (Prudential), James Kittley (boot and shoe maker), D. Lewis & Son (grocers and butchers), A. Lloyd, David Michael (greengrocer), Griffith Michael (ironmonger, jeweller, oil and furniture), James Mills, S. Morgan (grocer), T. Morgan (grocer and butcher), Thos Morgan (butcher), J. Nevill, B. Phillips (barber), M. Phillips, P. Ransom (chimney sweep), S. Rees (draper), W. Richards (barber), A. Saunders (china), H. Smith (flannel dealer), A. & E. Treharne (dress makers), G. Thomas (groceries and beer), J. Thomas, M.J. Thomas (butcher), T. Thomas (stationer), W. Thomas, David Vaughan (hardware), David Walters (butcher), David Ward (blacksmith), Griffith Williams (tailor), Wm Williams (coffee tavern), W. Williams (grocer), Benj Yearsley.

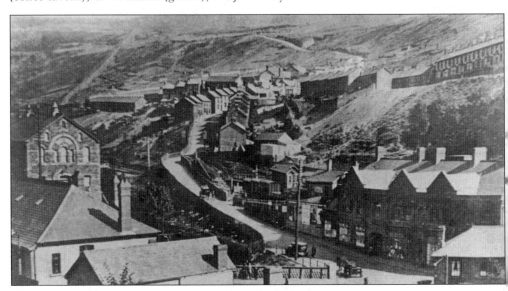

Pontygwaith Bridge and Stanleytown in the 1930s.

Left: Sergeant Bill John, Army Cadets, August 1946. *Right*: W.A. Thatcher Rubber Moulders drinking mug. W.A. Thatcher, affectionately known as the rubber factory, was built with Rest Assured, the bed manufacturers, in 1949.

Fernvale Brewery workmen in the 1950s. The Fernvale Brewery, Pontygwaith, supplied the pubs and clubs of the area. Pontygwaith also had two hotels, the Penrhys and the Bridgend; a cinema, called 'The Cosy' but fondly nicknamed 'The Bug'; a club in Furnace Road affectionately known as 'The Gluepot' because once men got in there they never seemed to come out. All these buildings have now been demolished.

Left: Pontygwaith Non-Political Club and Institute, twenty-first anniversary 6 Feb 1960. Top row, left to right: Jack Facey, Thomas Pritchard, Essex Mardon. Middle row: Horace Collier (secretary), Kenneth Mead (chairman), Stanley Thomas (vice chairman). Bottom row: George Williams, Arthur Richardson, Eddie Shipway (steward). *Right*: one-year-old Emily Louise Hobbs waiting for Queen Elizabeth II on her Golden Jubilee tour, 13 June 2002.

Her Majesty Queen Elizabeth II passing through Pontygwaith on her Golden Jubilee tour, 13 June 2002.

Pontygwaith residents celebrating the Queen's Golden Jubilee, 13 June 2002. Pontygwaith Community Centre, in the photograph, was officially opened on 29 March 1999. The activities programme includes a pre-school playgroup, tea dance, Girl Guides, computers, arts and crafts, action team for jobs, bingo, life skills integration, over-fifties club, slimming club, youth clubs, church group, Women's Institute and drop-in café.

Pontygwaith residents Mr Ronald Street and Mr Clarence Wooley celebrating the Queen's Golden Jubilee on 13 June 2002. Ron and Clarence represented the Pontygwaith Senior Citizens Group and met Her Majesty Queen Elizabeth II at the Rhondda Heritage Park.

A view of Pontygwaith in 1956.

A very rare lamp check from Pontygwaith Colliery. No. 8 Colliery Cynllwyn-du South was locally known and called Pontygwaith Colliery at the beginning of the twentieth century. Sinking of the pit began in 1858. The venture failed after a short time and sinking was also twice interrupted by strikes. The working rites were then purchased by David Davis, but remained idle until 1892 when the pit was reopened and sunk to the deeper seams.

Pontygwaith Senior Citizens Group at the Cosmo in 2001. Left to right, back row: Bill Perkins, John Scobie (local correspondent for the *Rhondda Leader*), John Leach, Vernon Owen, Irene Jones, Mavis Faulkner, Graham Jones. Front row: Howell Thomas, Albert Faulkner. The group meets every Tuesday afternoon in the lounge at the Cosmo.

Pontygwaith Senior Citizens Group at the Cosmo in 2001. Left to right: Jill Gronno, Joyce Newton, Dennis Morris, Pat Morris, Lucy Facey, Doreen Faulkner, Bernard Jones, George Baker. Among the group's favourite pastimes are bingo, seaside and historical outings, the theatre, holidays in the Isle of Wight and special Christmas concerts.

Pontygwaith Junior School teaching staff in 1931. The photograph includes Mr D.T. Davies (headteacher), Miss Gamble, Mr Anthony Davies, Mr Thomas and Mr Edwin Edwards.

Pontygwaith Junior School in 1955. The infant school opened on 30 October 1893, and the junior school opened on 4 February 1896. The photograph includes Mrs Nellie 'Farm' Lewis (teacher), Lynda Walters, Lesley Jones (Hughes) and Pamela Dally.

Ysgol Gymraeg Pontygwaith (Pontygwaith Welsh School) in 1955. The Welsh school at Pontygwaith, Ysgol Gymraeg y Rhondda Fach, was opened on 6 September 1950. The number of pupils on that first day was thirteen. By 1960 the number had risen to fifty. There were seventy-five in 1967 and 105 in 1969, and in 1971, on the occasion of the twenty-first anniversary, the number of pupils was 135. Ysgol Gymraeg Pontygwaith closed in 1980.

Ysgol Gymraeg Pontygwaith in 1966. Left to right, back row: Mrs Doris Davies (headteacher), Alun Jones, Cledwyn Merriman, Colin Bailey, Telor James, Mrs Ceinwen Green (teacher). Middle row: Michael Thomas, Christine Rees, Susan Thomas, Colleen ?, Front row: Jacqueline Davies, Janet Palfrey, Helen Evans, Siân Burton, Ann Evans.

A view of Pen-Yr-Heol Farm and Stanleytown from Old Smokey Tip above the village. Stanleytown is thought to have been named after the Welsh explorer, Henry Morton Stanley 1841-1904. The mainstay of every Rhondda farmer was the raising of sheep and, on a more limited scale, cattle. The Rhondda breed of sheep, though small in size, was quick and nimble and well adapted to local conditions of terrain, soil and climate. The plateau slopes along the valleys of the Rhondda rivers and their tributaries provided immense runs for thousands of sheep.

A view of Pen-Yr-Heol Farm from Old Smokey Tip. The farm is on the road leading to Llanwynno and is now the home of Chris Bryant MP. Most farms at the beginning of the nineteenth century were located close to rivers, or at points on the hillside near springs. These low, thatched or tiled, thick-walled farms dotted the wooded slopes of the Upper Rhondda Fach, and at this time the only place where there was a small cluster of labourers' cottages was Pontygwaith.

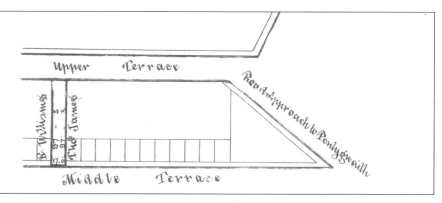

A plan of 12 Middle Terrace, Stanleytown, 12 March 1895. From the deed: 'Now in the course of erection, except and always reserved out of this demise to the person or persons for the time being entitled to the said premises in reversion expectant upon the expiration or determination of the term hereby granted (hereinafter called 'the Reversioner or Reversioners') all mines seams, veins and beds of coal, lead or iron ore blackband, stone gravel, marl sand and clay and all other mines minerals and other earthy substances of what nature and kind soever lying in upon or under the said piece of land hereby demised or any part thereof. (All mineral rites [sic] remain the property of the coalowner).' Gwyn Richards kindly supplied the above plan and information.

osh (left), Catherine and Evan Evans. Evan 'Chippo' and Catherine Evans were the first to move into 12 Middle Terrace, Stanleytown, when it was built. The deeds read: 'Dated 12th March 1895, No. 53 Pen-Yr-Heol Farm (12 Middle Terrace). Mrs Clara J.I.B. Gordon Canning, and Mrs Augusta E.S. Curre, and the Trustees of the Will of Crawshay Bailey, Esq, Deceased, Mr Evan Evans, Counterpart Building Lease of a parcel of land, situate in the parish of Llanwonno in the county of Glamorgan.' He purchased the house and land, comprising 100 square feet, for £75. (Photograph Byron Thomas).

Stanleytown soup kitchen in 1926. The photograph includes Gina Watkins, Catherine Evans, Nora Phillips, Mrs Hughes (of 3 Middle Terrace), Tom Roberts, Mrs Lynam and Will 'Chippo' Evans. Most of the houses were built in 1904 to accommodate miners for the local collieries.

Upper Terrace, Stanleytown, in 1927. The photograph includes Hazel White, Myra Jones and Gwyn Jones. The keys to the houses in Stanleytown were entrusted to the safe keeping of Evan 'Chippo' Evans prior to the families moving into their new homes. Many of the streets in the Rhondda were named after the coalowners or their children, others were named after their villages

Stanleytown outing to Porthcawl in 1934. The photograph includes Jack Jones, Dennis Thomas, Vernon Thomas, Annie Jones, Mrs and Mrs Jones (36 Middle Terrace), George Henry Jones, Joan Vowes, Mr and Mrs Osborne, Albert Jones, David and Katie Thomas, Catherine Evans, Mary and Noel Thomas, Emlyn Thomas and Will and Lillian Richards.

Stanleytown footbridge in 1947. The damage was caused by the harsh winter of 1946/47.

A sketch of the Stanley Hotel before demolition in 1976 by local artist Mr Ken Williams. The Stanley Hotel was originally named The Stanley Arms and was built in 1900; the Stanley was noted for having the best darts team in the area at the time. The pub was destroyed by fire on Monday 26 August 1976. Other businesses in the town to have closed include a post office, grocery shop, fish and chip shop.

Stanley Hotel darts team, league champions and winners of Ely Brewery Challenge Cup 1937/38 season. The photograph includes J. John, Will Harris, Alf Morgan, Mrs Payne (landlady), Mr Payne (landlord), Peggy Payne, Evan 'Grampy' Owen, Tom Roberts, Will Powell, Will 'Corporal' Williams, Evan 'Plaster' Jones, Nick Lock and Will Bateman.

Stanley Hotel drinking tankard.

Old Smokey in the snow.

Stanleytown ladies in 1950. The photograph includes Katie Thomas, Annie Jones, Velow Williams, Nora Phillips, Elsie Williams, Maggie May Evans, ninety-nine-year-old Lillian Richards and Maggie Vincent. The coal fire has always been a symbol of a warm welcome in the valleys and these ladies would bake bread and cakes, cook dinners and boil buckets of water for the bath in readiness for the miner on his return home from the pit covered in coal dust.

Councillor Carey Powell, who lived at Middle Terrace, Stanleytown, in 1969. Carey was born in 1902 and was a councillor from the mid-1950s until his death in 1970. He was awarded a British Empire Medal (BEM) in the mid-1960s for his services to the National Coal Board, he was a member of the Welsh Rugby Union and he became deputy mayor in 1970, the year he died. The Carey Day Centre for Senior Citizens, built in 1969, is named after him. Councillor Carey Powell was gracious, generous, compassionate and just to others, and lived his life as an offering of praise to God no matter where it led him.

A view from Stanleytown Bridge in the 1950s. Bottom right is a 56 Class locomotive and Lower Terrace can be seen top right in the photograph. The names for three streets in Stanleytown could not be agreed upon during the early stages of building and it was not until just before the occupants moved in that it was quickly decided to name the streets Lower, Middle and Upper Terrace.

A view from Stanleytown Bridge in 2002. Lower Terrace can be seen top right in the photograph. Stanleytown celebrated its centenary in 1994 and is now purely residential. The valleys are transformed from being the centre of heavy engineering and mining to being green and lush.

Stanleytown Infant School with Lala and baby Meryle Jones in 1948. Stanleytown Infant School was built in 1872. The eight houses built in 1997 on the former infant school site are called School Villas, named by John Scobie in memory of the school. The streets in Stanleytown are Llanwonno Road, Stanley Square, Lower, Middle and Upper Terrace; Pen-yr-Heol Road, leading to Pen-yr-Heol Farm; Llanwonno Road and Witherdene Road.

Stanleytown Infant School in 1934. The photograph includes Daisy Jones, Dylys Loosemoore, Miss Evans (teacher), Enid Brushfield, Betty Gummer, Eileen John, Robert Gilder, Glanville Roberts, Maldwyn Rogers, Gordon Howells, Byron Thomas, Eddie Beresford, Desmond Mathews, Ray Bents, Bertie Howring and Eidie Lewis.

Stanleytown Infant School children attend Tylorstown Primary School, 2002. Left to right, back row: Rachel Rogers, Mitchell Tann, Ieuan Pope, Craig Miles. Front row: Harry Griffiths, Kieran Tann, Louisa Williams, Shay Rees, Dylan Smith. Stanleytown, seen in the background, holds many fond and happy memories.

Stanleytown Junior School children attend Tylorstown Primary School, 2002, which provides good education thanks to headteacher Mrs Carol Basini, the staff and the support of the parents and families. Left to right: Saheera El-Jamel, Melisa Pope, Tessa Owen, Catherine Adams, Gemma Owen, Jarrad Brough, Jake Williams, Jarrad Griffiths, Richard Pope, Kyrie-El-Jamel, Amy Griffiths.

Our Lady of Penrhys. Penrhys is said to derive its name from the improbable tradition that Rhys ap Tewdwr, Prince of South Wales, was beheaded or taken prisoner there. The place is of particular historical significance, however, for here was erected an image to the Virgin Mary, and here also is St Mary's Well, which, like Lourdes, was reputed to have miraculous healing powers.

St Mary's Well, Ffynon Fair. Thousands of pilgrims came to receive the water from the ancient well and to pray at the statue on the brow of the hill. Legend tells us that the original statue of the Madonna, crowned and bearing Jesus in her arms, was grafted between branches of an oak tree. In the sixteenth century, the Reformers, believing that respect for Mary had become idolatry, stole the statue by night and burnt it publicly in Chelsea in 1538. Four hundred years later, on 2 July 1953, a new statue in Portland stone was erected and blessed.

The steep hill climb to Penrhys in 1954. This area of North Glamorgan is associated with three Celtic saints: Illtud, Gwynno and Tyfodwg. Their settlements were known as a 'llan'. Illtud, one of the founders of monasticism in Britain, was teacher of Dewi Sant (Saint David), our patron saint.

Penrhys in 1954 with Our Lady of Penrhys and Penrhys Uchaf Farm. It is on the site of the original altar of the Cistercian chapel, and a Cistercian abbot, Don Malachy Brasil of Mount St Bernard's, unveiled the new statue of Our Blessed Lady with a crown upon her head and 'nursing Jesus for a Kiss'. Penrhys had again become a place of pilgrims and hospitality.

Penrhys Uchaf Farm in the harsh snowy winter of 1964. The farmer had to grow crops for domestic use. Corn was generally grown in the more fertile fields on the flat meadowland, but the narrow Cwm Rhondda Fach was by no means as fortunate as Cwm Rhonda Fawr. (Photograph J.H. Davies).

Left: Snow-covered churns of milk ready for delivery in 1964. The hardy cattle of the valleys – red-brown in colour with speckled faces – bore considerably the features of those of the vale, but due to the breed having been kept more pure, without crossing, and being housed in winter, the cattle are of a more compact shape, deeper-chested, fuller in the flank, shorter legged and of a considerably smaller size. *Right*: The joy of spring. (Photographs J.H. Davies).

A group of friends in Penrhys, 1997. Left to right: Morus Williams, Thomas Williams, Neil Griffiths. The community of Penrhys enjoys more than average sunlight – and winds of Hebridean velocity. It has replaced its medieval fame with a notoriety caused by the excesses of 1960s planners.

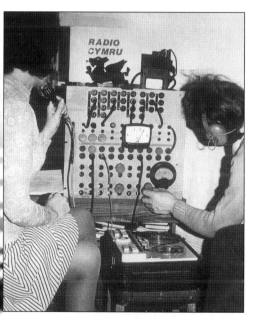

Left: Hawys and Glyn James broadcasting on the first 'pirate radio' in South Wales at Penrhys Uchaf Farm in 1958. 'Peidiwch â throi eich teledu i ffwrdd pan ddaw'r amser i gau i lawr,' they would tell listeners ('Don't switch off at close-down. Listen to Radio Wales'). *Right*: Penrhys, a community to which people wish to belong, is situated on top of a mountain that divides Rhondda Fawr and Rhondda Fach. It was officially opened on Friday 13 September 1968 with nearly 1,000 dwellings, which rise from 1,000 to 1,350 ft.

A view of Penrhys from Old Smokey Tip in 1966.

A view of Penrhys from Old Smokey Tip in 1970. Field and meadow names in the area include Erw Penyrhiw (acre at the top of the hill), Y Fynwent (the graveyard), Cae'r Eglwys (Church field), Cae Tyla Capel (the field of the slope of the chapel), Erw Porth (gate acre), Cae gwar yr heol (the field on the shoulder of the road), Cae Newydd (new field) and Cae Cefn (back field).

The chapel at Penrhys is called Llanfair – Mary's Community, Mary's settlement, Mary's people, Mary's church. And to deepen the sense of God's providential guidance through the centuries, the church bell was a gift from the Cistercian monks of Caldey Island. The bell that once rang from the ancient parish church of Saint Mary on the seashore at Caldey now rings at Saint Mary's on the mountain at Penrhys.

Pendyrus RAOB (Rhondda Ancient Order of Buffaloes) Lodge in 1979. Left to right, back row: J. Portt, W. Owen, G. Hooker, A. Portt, D. Bethel, M. Bennett. Front row: G. Watkins, B. Owen, A. Hawkins. The Pendyrus RAOB Lodge 9963 was founded on 21 July 1974 at The Penrhys pub and moved to the purpose-built Pendyrus Social Club – the 'Buff Club' – in April 1985. The Buffs are known for helping many charities including ill and disabled children.

Golfers John Davies and Anthony Jones at the Rhondda Golf Club, Penrhys, in 2000. Probably the most famous valley in the world, Cwm Rhondda has many attractions for today's visitor including the Rhondda Golf Club at Penrhys, which was founded and officially opened in 1910.

The Rhondda Golf Club has staged the Welsh Masters tournament and is the only member's club in Wales to stage a three-day event continuously over a seven-year period. During this time the club has impressed many visitors who have enjoyed a good golf course, panoramic views and the tremendous legendary Rhondda hospitality, which is very much in evidence at the club; visitors will always receive a warm welcome.

The eighteen holes on the golf course are named after the following Rhondda collieries: 1 Tydraw, 2 Parc and Dare, 3 Pentre, 4 Gelli, 5 Glamorgan, 6 Cambrian, 7 Naval, 8 Dinas, 9 Cymmer, 10 Lewis Merthyr, 11 Bodringallt, 12 Standard, 13 Cynllwyn-du, 14 National, 15 Pendyrus, 16 Pontygwaith, 17 Tylorstown, 18 Mardy.

The presidents: Sir L.W. Llewellyn, Mr G. Davies, Mr W.N. Thomas, Mr D.M. Morgan, 1994 Rt Hon Viscount Tonypandy, 1998 Mr R.F. Morgan. The first captain was Dr J.D. Jenkins 1910-1920 and Mr P. Lott for 2000 the new millennium.

Seniors champions: 1992 Mr D. Wilkins, 1993 K. Addis, 1994 M. Smith, 1995 D. Chapman, 1996 A.I. Brown, 1997 M. Smith, 1998 M. Smith, 1999 Mal Evans, 2000 J. Davies, 2001 D. Alforn.

Penrhys Athletic AFC in 1992. Left to right, back row: Christopher Hill, Stephan Bartlett, Alan Moss, Jamie Lewis, Johnny Derrick, Phillip Eason, Raymond Williams, David Thomas, Stephan Cavill. Front row: Gareth Hurton (captain), Andrew Mitchell, Cêri Mathias, Ivor Williams, Jamie Ellis, Martin ?. Penrhys Athletic AFC won the Agnes John Rhondda and District Football League title in 2002. Penrhys Athletic AFC was formed and joined the Rhondda league in 1990, and is sponsored by Penrhys RAOB.

Waiting for Her Majesty Queen Elizabeth II on her Golden Jubilee tour, 13 June 2002. The Penrhys housing project seen in the background, designed by Alex Robertson, Peter Francis & Partners, Cardiff, was officially completed and opened on Friday 13 September 1968. It was built by George Wimpey & Company and heated by a central boiler house operated by the National Coal Board.

Penrhys Tŷr Gwaidd nursery school in 2001. There have been two headteachers since the school opened on 5 March 1973: Mrs Beryl Roach between 1969 and 1985 and Miss Bethan Williams from 1985 to 2001. Penrhys Tyr Gwaidd nursery closed on 24 July 2001.

Penrhys Junior School in 1973. The photograph includes Mrs Henshaw (headteacher), Stephan Cooper, Michael Dibbings, Raymond Williams, Alan Wilding, Robert Stephens, Ivor Jones, Stephan Jacker, Danny Morgan, Gerald Griffiths, Lee Joes, Royston Jenkins, Leslie Debinet, Kay Fisher, David Joseph Jones, Deon Pearce, Andrew 'Lump' Lawrence, Yvonne Sandri, Julie Bowen, Corinne Jones, Diane Williams, Paula Bents, Julie Reed, Michael Llewellyn, Vanessa Griffiths, Sharon Dobbs, Jackie Kennedy, Carl Richardson, Gary Roberts, Mark Jones and Royston Pugh.

Penrhys Junior School, 11 June 1987. The school opened on 3 September 1970.

Penrhys Junior School pupils on a visit to Big Pit Mining Museum, 2 April 1990. Penrhys School has built for itself a fine reputation for good education and this is due to the dedication of the staff, the willingness of the pupils and the support of the parents and families in the community. From 1 January 2003 all nursery, infants and junior pupils will be accommodated at the junior school.

My Dad

I often look back through the years although some days were sad
But I have happy memories of my beloved Dad.
It seems like only yesterday Dad held me on his knee
He'd tell such funny stories and I would laugh with glee.
He worked so very hard for us, we were his pride and joy,
I was his only little girl and Glyn his only boy.
He was so kind and gentle so good in every way
And as the years go drifting on I miss him more each day.
Dad loved his little organ, he played it every day,
I often sat and listened and wished that I could play.
There came the day my wish came true and this I must confess
The joys I've had in playing I owe to my Aunt Bess.
Dad came with me to practice to teach me how to chant
For I became the organist in Eglwys Dewi Sant.

To the memory of my loving father, who died 18 May 1952. Mally Jones

Cwm Rhondda Sheep

When I was a child, I always felt sorry for sheep – the ewes that is, not the head-butting, cheeky rams. The ewes had woebegone looks on their thin, grubby faces as they wandered disconsolately from street to street and through back 'gwlis' (lanes) scrounging and foraging for food. The Rhondda sheep were a bedraggled, coal-dusty crew with their woollen coats matted and some parts hanging unevenly down like dirty, tattered dresses.

Sheep were as much a part of our lives as the pit hooters, pigeon cotes and 'Bracchi' shops and most people threw their vegetable peelings and stale bread in the 'gwlis' for them. They always seemed to be hungry, especially in winter-time when the snow was on the ground and they'd eat practically anything, even newspapers that had been wrapped around fish-shop fish and chips.

Mam always peeled potatoes and some vegetables on Saturday evening for our Sunday lunch and I used to remind her to keep the peelings for the sheep, especially in the winter-time. I remember one Sunday morning in particular – it was snowing and when I looked out of the front window I could see a small flock of ewes huddled together against the wall in the biting winds and driving snow. Mam put the peelings in a pan for my older sister to take out to the sheep but I insisted on going to feed them myself. I put on my coat and hat and felt very important and grown up as I cautiously made my way down the slippery steps of our house with my hands tightly gripping the edges of the pan. I opened our gate at the bottom of the steps and stood in the snow holding out the pan and making encouraging clicking sounds. The small flock quickly spotted me and stampeded in my direction. I stood as if mesmerised by the suddenness of the onslaught, the pan still in my hands.

A big ewe reached me first and thrust her front legs up on my shoulders with such force that I staggered. Other sheep surrounded me, jostling and bleating and wild for food. I tried to keep my footing but I slithered and fell on to my back in the snow with my feet up in the air, the pan still in my hands and all the sheep looking down at me trying to get at their food while their breath rose like steam in the icy air and their bulging eyes were so close to mine. I can still remember the strong smell of their wet wool like damp, musty old rags. Luckily, my laughing sister rescued me and carried me, sobbing and wet, into the house.

Hawys Glyn James

Three
Tylorstown, Ferndale, Blaenllechau, Llanwynno, Maerdy

In 1872 the mineral rights of Pendyrus lands were bought by Alfred Tylor, after whom Tylorstown was named, and in 1873 the sinking of No. 6 and No. 7 shafts began. Great difficulties were encountered and it was not until 1876 that the steam coal seams were won. Coal was first dispatched to Cardiff in January 1877 and subsequently, under the direction of Herbert Kirkhouse, the development of the Pendyrus Colliery was extremely rapid, output increasing from 3,252 tons in 1877 to 241,061 tons in 1893.

When sinking the pit commenced at Ferndale in 1857, there were but a few farmhouses in the locality: Blaenllechau and Nant-dyrys in the parish of Llanwynno; Ffaldau in the parish of Aberdare; Duffryn Sarfwch and Rhondda Fechan in the parish of Ystradyfodwg. Immediately the steam coal seams were won, advertisements appeared in the press offering work at Ferndale. At first, the difficulty of accommodating the workers and their families was a serious one. The original sinkers, about forty in number, had been housed as one community in a single dwelling house, 'Y Lluest', while the first miners and their families were accommodated in wooden huts called the 'barracks'.

On Saturday 16 November 1867 a journalist wrote in the *Merthyr Express*: 'Blaenllechau of Ferndale as it is known by the name of the Colliery, is a wild region situated at the top of the Rhondda Fach, one of the most beautiful little valleys in South Wales, as tortuous as the valley of the Wye between Ross and Chepstow, in some places not more than 80 yards wide, with all the sides covered in Welsh Oak trees and the torten of the Little Rhondda running a chequered and uneven course along the bed.'

Nestling in the lee of bleak, windswept Cefn Gwyngul, a short leisurely stroll from Club Row, Blaenllechau, between the Rhondda Fach and the Cynon valleys, the parish church of Llanwynno looks out upon the surrounding hills as if it were the apparent last outpost of civilization, though the public house which stands no more than twenty yards away might claim this distinction for itself with equal vigour and possibly more support. Yet, despite its isolated situation, Eglwyswynno possesses an interesting past, for the church, dating back to the twelfth century, was at one time the centre of one of the most important parishes in Glamorgan.

The village of Maerdy grew around the economic prosperity that came from the 'Black Gold' produced by Mardy No. 1 and No. 2 Collieries, and by the late 1870s the village had begun to hold religious services at the Maerdy farmhouse. Neighbouring farmers and shepherds assembled here to conduct important business transactions and attend the court of the district. The occupier of the farm was the president of the court, hence the title 'Maerdy' the steward's or mayor's house.

Tylorstown No. 8 and No. 9 Colliery in 1906. Sinking of Cynllwyn-du No. 8 South Pit, also known as Pontygwaith Pit, began in 1858.

Y Dryw (undermanager) at Cynllwyn-du Colliery No. 8 South Pit in 1906. The inscription reads: 'D. Davis and Sons, Cynllwyn-du Colliery No. 8 Pit, weight 31cwt' [1,578 kilos]. The colliery was owned by the Powell Duffryn Steam Coal Company prior to nationalization in 1947.

Left: James Edwards' safety lamp. James died in the explosion that occurred at Tylorstown Colliery on 28 January 1896 just after 5.30 a.m. causing the deaths of fifty-seven miners. James had three sons, Thomas, Evan and Ted. Thomas the youngest had two children, a son and a daughter. The son has died, but the daughter is still living. *Right*: The colliery electric power station in 1906.

Left: Shackled in comradeship outside No. 9 Colliery blacksmith's shop in 1953. Left to right: craftsmen Dai 'Wara' Williams, Phillip Quick and Danny James. *Right*: Left to right: craftsmen Gwyn Evans, Glyn 'Sharkey' Jones, Stan Williams, Brian Jones and Phillip Quick in 1958. Tylorstown No. 8 and No. 9 Colliery was closed by the NCB on Friday 15 October 1960.

Pendyrus (Tylorstown) No. 6 and No. 7 Colliery in 1958. Back row, centre, is Thomas Charles Ellis (1905-1986), and the dog at the front is his faithful companion Kim. In 1876, at a depth of 333 yards, the steam coal seams were won. In 1915 the No. 6 pit employed 617 men and the No. 7 pit employed 1,024 men. The colliery ceased coaling in 1936 and was retained for pumping and ventilation, finally closing along with the No. 8 and No. 9 Colliery on 15 October 1960 by the NCB.

Tylorstown Ambulance Brigade in 1906 with Dr S. Glanville Morris, chief surgeon for the Mardy collieries and compiler of the first addition of the First Aid Manual. Mardy No. 1 Squad became famous as the holders of the Sir C. Warren's Rhondda Shield, the Glamorgan County Shield and the Provincial White Horse Shield, besides being holder of three champion cups and eight gold and silver medals.

Remains of Tylorstown No. 8 and No. 9 Colliery in 1969. Today, below the Jubilee Hotel in the centre of the photograph is Lidl supermarket and a memorial for Tylorstown No. 8 and No. 9 Colliery which was unveiled on 3 September 1999 by Peter Cloke (Groundwork Merthyr & Rhondda Cynon Taff) and the Mid Fach River Care Group. The river walk below, under the care of MFCG, is now a beauty spot, attracting many visitors to the area.

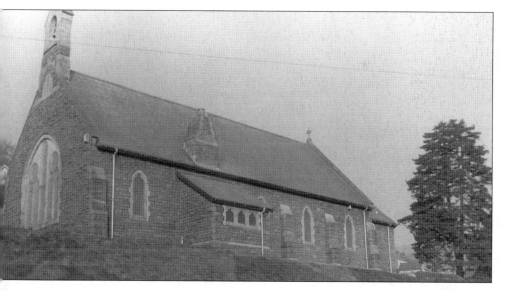

Holy Trinity church, Tylorstown, was erected in 1883 at a cost of £1,400 and is a building of Welsh sandstone with Bath stone dressings, consisting of chancel, nave and a western turret containing one bell. In 1887 Holy Trinity Church, Tylorstown, together with Ferndale and Maerdy, was formed into an ecclesiastical parish, but in 1900 Ferndale and Maerdy were separated from Tylorstown and reconstituted as a distinct parish. In 1903 a new vestry for the church was built and an organ provided.

Tylorstown No. 8 and No. 9 Colliery rugby team in the 1950s. The photograph includes Carey Powell, B. Bateman, Maldwyn James (colliery manager), Tom Wigley, Bob Sedgwick, Stan Howells, Tom 'Sally' Williams, Eddie Phillips, Dennis Bonnell (under-manager), Owen Hughes, Hubert John (NCB), B. Gully, K. Davies, B. Rees and H. Davies.

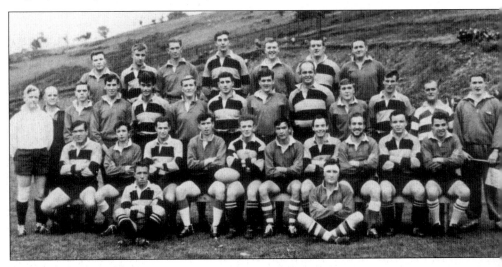

Tylorstown RFC rugby team in 1964. The photograph includes B. Maslin, G. Griffin, B. Wilde, J. Evans, M. Bent, N. Johnson, John Bowden, T. Anthony (referee), S. Howells, A. Wilde, G. Hughes, A. Evans, G. Thomas, C. Boulter, R. Williams, Ian Ford (Wales), G. Biddle, K. Poo, Roy Taylor, A. Jones, B. Meredith (Wales and Lions), N. Cox, R. Cheney, A. Clement, R. Rosser (captain), B. Condon, D. Perrott, M. Brough, G. Bevan, W. Davies, I. Taylor and P. Quick. 2003 is the centenary year of Tylorstown RFC.

Tylorstown Working Men's Club & Institute committee in 1987. Left to right, back row: Tommy 'Yorkie' Williams (vice chairman), Ray Price, Andy Lewis, Keith Winder, Dai Hooper, Peter Jenkins, Emlyn 'Bing' Jones (entertainment secretary), Richard 'Dick the Milk' Lewis, Mike Bradley. Front row: John 'Boxer' Williams (chairman), Gilbert Bevan (secretary), Mrs Pat Rees (mayoress), Lynda Grocott (stewardess), John Grocott (steward), Sam Winder (treasurer), Mr Gwyn Rees (mayor), Mervyn 'Mighty Mouse' Watkins, Elfed Davies.

Tylorstown Senior Citizens Group in 2002. Left to right, back row: Barbara England, Gwladys Jenkins, Len Melhuish, Elfed Davies, Ivor Rees, Trefor Lewis, Glyn Thomas, Joyce Thomas, Morfydd Lewis. Front row: Gordon Stokes, Idrissa Stokes.

Tylorstown Hendrefadog Girls School standard 2a in 1928. The photograph includes Mally Jones, Iris May, Tydful Lewis, Morfydd Jones, Lillian Harris and Miss Dosie Scorfield (teacher). Tylorstown Hendrefadog senior boys, girls and infants schools were built in 1879-89 by Alban Richards and were affectionately known as 'the academy on the hill'.

Tylorstown Hendrefadog Girls School form 2b sports-winning team in 1951. The photograph includes Mr Davies (headteacher), Miss Chivers (teacher), Eileen Thomas, Eirion Jones, Brenda ?, Margaret Lewis, Glenys ?, Sheila Walters, Glenys Swift and Pat Lewis. The first school in Tylorstown was held at No. 11 and No. 12 East Road.

Tylorstown Primary School (Ysgol Gynradd Tylorstown) 17 April 2002. Headteacher Mrs Carol Basini rings the bell for the pupils' first day in their brand new school. Councillor Robert Bevan said, 'What a great day for everyone connected to the school. What a brilliant new school for the local community'. The old primary school opened in 1880.

Tylorstown Primary School (Ysgol Gynradd Tylorstown) nursery class, 17 April 2002. A fire completely destroyed the school on Thursday 29 June 2000. The school opened in temporary accommodation units on 2 October 2000. The pupils returned to the new school after the Easter holidays on 17 April 2002.

Ferndale (Glynrhedynog) No. 1 and No. 5 Colliery in 1954. In August 1862, the first load of steam coal was sent from Ferndale to Cardiff and the industrial era of the Rhondda Fach had begun. On Friday 15 July 1988 a memorial for the Ferndale Collieries was unveiled in memory of the 178 miners who lost their lives on 10 June 1867 and the fifty-three miners who lost their lives on 8 November 1869 at Ferndale No.1 Pit. Ferndale No. 1 and No. 5 Colliery was closed on 29 August 1959 by the NCB.

 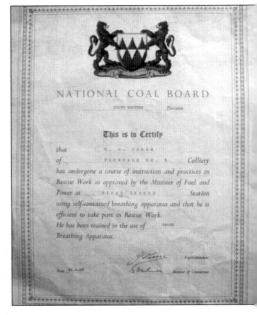

Left: Ferndale Colliery horse brass. If coal was king in the valleys then the horse was the prince. *Right*: NCB certificate awarded to Kerrigan Jones on 29 March 1957. It certifies that he has been trained to undertake rescue work.

Ferndale No. 2 and No. 4 Colliery in 1906. The colliery, locally known as Ffaldau Pits, was sunk in 1870 by David Davis and Sons. The Four-Feet seam was at a depth of 667ft, Lower Six-Feet at 741ft, Upper Nine-Feet at 823ft, Lower Nine-Feet at 850ft, Yard at 923ft, Middle Seven-Feet at 961ft, Five-Feet at 1,008ft, Gellideg at 1,027ft and sunk to 1,050ft. Ferndale No. 2 and No. 4 Colliery closed in 1930.

The funeral of the late Mr Murray (bandsman) proceeding from the top of North Road towards the cemetery in the late nineteenth century. The first burial at the cemetery was David William Morgan, the son of collier David Morgan, on 30 May 1877. The houses on the right in the photograph are the White Huts and there is no Morris Terrace or Parade.

Trerhondda chapel Cantata in the 1940s. Trerhondda chapel foundation stone was laid on 15 July 1867 by Master William Lloyd Davis, Maesyffynon. In 1990 Trerhondda chapel was reopened with the arts factory underway. Facilities include a toddlers playgroup and classes in computer skills, art, music, keep fit, craft, karate, creative writing etc.

Left: Ferndale Wesley Methodist chapel opened in 1880, but was destroyed by fire in 1891. Lewis Davis, coalowner, died 1 January 1888 and his wife, children and friends rebuilt Ferndale Wesley Methodist chapel in memory of him in 1893 with seating accommodation for 350. The chapel was demolished in 1986 and a new Wesley Methodist chapel was built and opened on Saturday 10 March 1990. *Right*: Wesley Methodist chapel Sunday school banner.

Left: Salem Newydd Welsh Baptist chapel was officially opened on 30-31 December 1877 at a cost of £2,046 7s 6d. *Right*: Harpist Edwin Richards and his son Glyndwr in 1910. The words 'This is how we amused ourselves' are written on the back of the photograph. The harp was presented to Ferndale Grammar School in 1958.

The first tram arrives at Ferndale Strand, 11 July 1908. Considering the alpine nature of the route from Porth through some of the switchback roads, it was a feat not to be sneered at and some of the tram journeys proved unexpectedly exciting for the travellers. Travel was difficult as pits were in existence long before this and miners found themselves trekking great distances to neighbouring pits. For many, the everyday means of transport was the bicycle.

A view of Ferndale with Christ Church in 1920. In 1887 Christ Church, together with Tylorstown and Maerdy, was formed into an ecclesiastical parish, but in 1900 it was separated from Tylorstown and together with Maerdy was formed into a new one under the name of Ferndale. The church was erected in 1887 at a cost of £2,237; it was built of Welsh sandstone with Bath stone dressings, and consisted of chancel, nave and a turret at the north end, which contained one bell. There was seating accommodation for 400.

Côr Meibion Morlais Choir in 1976. The photograph includes G. Jones, G. Mason, J. Williams, L. Huzzle, T. Jeffreys (conductor), B. Davies (accompanist), R. Condon, G. Baber, A. Collier, C. Francis, E. Evans and S. Clove. In February 1928, Alfred J. Morgan rehearsed his little glee group the 'Mustard Club'. The first occasion on which the name 'Morlais Glee Singers' was used was the choosing of a name for 'Alfie' Morgan. His father was a Dowlais man so the appellation 'Morlais' was a familiar one to him, as it was to all Merthyr people. The choir's first major success was at the Pontypridd Eisteddfod on 7 February 1929; the Morlais took first prize.

Ferndale Male Voice Choir, national champions in 1956. The photograph includes A. Williams (chairman), Bill Syms, Dai Thomas, Len Morris, 'Boyo' Hurton, Handel Thomas, Gwyn Edwards, Ronnie Leach, Jackie 'singer' Price, Jon Evans, Evan Thomas, Glyn Walters, Joe Cox, Alwyn Jenkins, Ivor Davies (accompanist), Haydn Alen (with cup), Bill 'Darkie' Jones, Fred Clements, Pat Condon, Ronnie Thomas, Ken Lewis, Edgar Williams. Ferndale Male Voice Choir was founded in 1949 in the Imperial Club by members Dai and Malwyn Thomas, Will Roberts and Tec Ellis Williams.

Ferndale Labour Club Melville Singers in 1962. The photograph includes Bryn 'Badger' Davies, Glan Walters, Harry Griffiths, Will Howells, Tom Protheroe, Martin Jeffries, Will 'Farm' Davies, Dai 'Top Note' Thomas, Peter Griffiths, Will John Griffiths, Dan Jeffries, Will John Jeffries, Brynmor Jones, Jack Lewis, Jobbie Davies and Dai 'Trig' Davies.

Ferndale Motor Cycle and Car Club at Rhondda Fechan Farm, Ferndale, in 1951. Left to right: Gwyn Lewis, Dai Philpot, Elfed Davies, Ron Richardson, Charlie Marsh, Fred Gregory, August Velcourt, Gwyn Thomas, Syd Martin, Ron Evans, Gwernydd Pritchard, Ken Hobbs, Joe Tibbles, Norman Botting (chairman), Bryn Roberts (secretary), George Rye, Colin Evans, Hubert Griffiths, -?-, Glyn Palfrey, Viv Thomas, Eric Marsh, Reg Jennings, Sam 'Farm' Evans, Trefor Radcliffe.

Rhondda Welsh Guards in 1955. The photograph includes Rhydian Gammon, Ken Arthur, Cyril Griffiths and Ivon Ellis. Rhondda's record as a reception area during the Second World War is one that will be remembered for all time. The homes of the people were thrown open to those less fortunate persons who were compelled to seek rest and shelter from the heavily bombed areas.

Her Majesty Queen Elizabeth II and HRH Duke of Edinburgh in 1989. Rhondda Housing Association was formed in 1979 to help combat the bad housing conditions existing in Rhondda. The first meeting was held at Ferndale Workmen's Hall. The photograph includes Her Majesty Queen Elizabeth II, HRH Duke of Edinburgh, John Allen, Alan Rogers MP, Lord Lieutenant of Glamorgan; Mrs Evans, Gwyn Evans (chief executive of Rhondda Borough Council), Irene and Selwyn Baber, Gwilym Lewis, Edith May Evans and Malcolm Fisk (chairman RHA 1989).

Ferndale Clinic staff on the day of closure 8 November 2000. The photograph includes Sue Sapoli, Margaret Evans, Andrea Coombes, Lisa Williams, Rian Lang, Sharon Jones, June Thomas, Lyndis Owen, Elaine Scammel, Sharon Davies, Jan Symmons, a student nurse (as yet unidentified), Jan Evans, Nathan Evans, Elaine Edwards, Joan Thomas, Carol Evans, Liz Conway and Mavis Row.

Ferndale & District Junior Association Football League. Ferndale Secondary School Juniors, undefeated champions, 1926-27 season. Left to right, back row: Jim Owen, Gwyn Rhydderch, V. Malpass, K. Ellis, W. Jones, C. Thomas. Middle row: Mr Rhys Jones BA (sports teacher), G. Weaver, Tom Roberts (captain), Elwyn Thomas, Mr G. Childs BSc (head teacher). Front row: Reg Roberts, Glyn Davies, Harold Ball, G. Oliver.

Ferndale Boys School sports team in 1945. The photograph includes Islwyn Thomas, G. Harrison, Vince Protheroe, William John Griffiths (sports teacher), L. Reynish, A. Lea, J. Condon, G. Thomas, John King, G. Evans, Glan Thomas and W. Jenkins.

Ferndale Dyffryn Girls School form 1 in 1968. The photograph includes Alison Vaughan, Margaret Screech, Maria Kozuh, Shelley James, Miss Elizabeth Mary Humphreys BA (head teacher), Helen Parker, Helen Davies, Barbara Wilcox, Ann Abbott, Mrs Hawys James (teacher), Kim Smith, Julie Lewis, Lynne Rossiter and Sharon Kibble. Dyffryn School opened in July 1903.

Ferndale Dyffryn Girls School form 4 in 1971. Left to right, back row: Karen Minton, Elaine Williams, Marion Hughes, Corrine Morris, Susan Kisby, Susan Lewis, Jackie L'Homme, Shirley Thomas. Middle row: Mrs Mary Shotton (teacher), Elaine Pike, Diane Anstey, Elizabeth Morris, Julie Harries, Joyce Lytton, Diane Mathews, Gillian Herbert, Mrs Elizabeth Mary Humphreys BA (head teacher). Front row: Llinos Thomas, Karen Jones, Janice Williams, Lynette Saunders, Alison Mcarthy, Christina ?, Susan Mathews.

Blaenllechau Farm in the new millennium. There is a stream at Blaenllechau called Nant Llechau, meaning head of the llechau. A llechau is a river flowing over slabs or flat rocks. A detailed report on Blaenllechau Farm shows how speculators' attention had been drawn to the mineral resources of the upper reaches of the Rhondda Fach in the mid-1840s; in November 1845, Thomas Thomas (alias Thomas Evans) offered to purchase the surface minerals and all rights of Blaenllechau Farm for £7,000.

A view of sunny Blaenllechau in 1956. Blaenllechau lies on the eastern side of the valley and has many attractions for today's visitor. 'Sunny Blaen' is the sunniest place in the Rhondda Fach, with its allotments and beautiful gardens and spectacular views overlooking Ferndale.

Left: The present-day Nazareth Welsh Baptist chapel was built in 1901 at a cost of £2,651 16s 6d and is situated at George Street, Blaenllechau. The first service was held on Sunday 13 April 1902. *Right*: Carmel Baptist chapel, Blaenllechau, was opened in 1870 and is now owned by the Presbyterian Church of Wales.

Carmel Baptist chapel Sunday school in 1970. The photograph includes Patricia Palmer (Sunday school teacher), Tracy Bond, Dean Owen, Amanda Williams, Wendy Williams, Mark Owen, Lee Burgoyne and Wendy Roberts (Sunday school teacher). For over 100 years many generations from the surrounding communities have met to worship at Carmel chapel. The induction of the Revd Owen Griffiths to the teaching and pastoral ministry took place on Saturday 7 September 2002.

Saint Thomas's church, Blaenllechau, opened 22 September 1918. The Reverend Neal Parfitt became Priest in charge of the Incumbency of Ferndale with Maerdy and Blaenllechau on 9 July 2002.

Ferndale and Blaenllechau town band in 1921. Blaenllechau annual sports, which were always accompanied by the band, were held at Ffaldau Farm and always attracted a large crowd of spectators and athletes. The main feature was the final of the 220-yard run, and the polo race was also a favourite event, with fifteen ponies usually taking part; the riders had to be very skilful at this sport. The money raised at these sport events was given to hospitals and other local institutions.

The Glynrhedynog Inn miners choir in 1926. One of the official choirs for the relief of miners wives and children during the 1926 strike. Fellow workers decided to support the miners and a general strike began on 3 May 1926. The strike lasted just nine days. The miners were eventually forced to accept the coalowners' terms and wage levels and returned to work on 1 December 1926.

Blaenllechau residents celebrating Her Majesty Queen Elizabeth II's Coronation in 1953. The photograph includes Carnival Queen Veronica Todd being crowned by Mrs Evans, Annie Tibbles, Elaine Moulds, Mair Roberts, Eileen Mason, Alun Evans, Roy Dutson, Viv Moulds and Bill Hennessey.

Co-op milkmen in 1953. The photograph includes Glyn Harrison, Glyn Evans, John Williams, Vince Protheroe, Dai Parry, Bryn Wiltshire, Glan Griffiths, Haydn Smith, Harold Stagg and David 'Dai Horse' Jones. Some of the milkmen went to the station early in the morning to meet the train and get churns of milk to supply their customers.

Blaen boys in 1960. Left to right: Eddie Thomas, Ieuan Gwyn, Leighton Gwyn (baby), Ivor Gwyn with faithful companion Pudge, Ieuanto Owen and Ivor 'Titch' England.

Radical Institute CIA skittle champions in 1963. Left to right: Ken 'Ginger' Davies, Ray Roberts, Billy England, Ronnie Jones and John Jenkins. Sport at Blaenllechau was always popular: quoits with pitches at the old quarry, Mountain Row, Club Row and pwll-lwyn; professional boxers, footballers, rugby players and athletes.

Taken during the 1984-85 miners' strike, this photograph includes NUM dispute agent Harry Coombs (left), Mary Coombs (centre), of the Miners Women's Support Group, and George Hickman. It was the longest strike in South Wales and British mining history. Within a week every South Wales miner was on strike and the South Wales Coalfield was to be the most solid for the duration of the year-long strike.

Blaenllechau Youth Drop-In, with disabled access, opened 21 July 2002. Left to right: Christopher Carter, Sean Dillon (youth development coordinator), David Williams (youth worker) and Garry Griffiths. Blaenllechau Youth Project works with five to twenty-five-year-old children in the Mid and Upper Rhondda Fach. It has three full-time youth workers, a pool table, a jukebox, a TV, video and DVD room and a computer room with internet access. It is open every day and three evenings a week, including school holidays.

The Bell Centre celebrating the Queen's Golden Jubilee, 10 June 2002. Left to right: Fay Rawbone, Bethan Evans, Rachel Chilcott, Laura Watkins, Elen Jenkins, Stephanie Bond, Mia Williams, Alys Clement, Hannah Jones, Kelsey Evans, Vicky Clement. The Bell Centre, (Blaenllechau Enterprise for Life-Long Learning), opened in September 1996.

Blaenllechau Infant School years one and two in 2002. Left to right: Amy Paul, Sacha Hobbs, Stephanie Lewis, Kirsty Smith, Ricky Price, David England, Hannah Holmes, Molly Gunton, Catharine Frances, Beth Williams, Georgia Carter, Kelsey Villis, Sophie Evans, Rachel Jenkins, Krishian Parry, Elouise Smith.

Blaenllechau Infants School years one and two in 2002. Left to right: Kieron Youset, Kieron Isaac, Ffion Thomas, Zach Lewis, Harry England, Connor Smith, Robyn Keetch, Rebecca Hester, Lucie Jones, Kayleigh Parry, Megan Griffiths, Laurenne Tavener, Isabel Grundy, Christian Carter. Blaenllechau Infants School opened in 1879.

Llanwynno (church of Saint Gwynno). Nestling in the lee of bleak, windswept Cefn Gwyngul, a short stroll from Club Row, Blaenllechau, between the Rhondda Fach and the Cynon Valleys, the parish church of Llanwynno looks out upon the surrounding hills as if it were the last outpost of civilization. Despite its isolated situation however, Eglwyswynno possesses an interesting past, for the church, which dates back to the twelfth century, was at one time the centre of one of the most important parishes in Glamorgan.

Who was Gwynno? He remains a very obscure character indeed. It has been suggested that he entered Britain during the Roman occupation, but this is highly unlikely. Gwynno appears to have been the son of Cau, called Euryn y Coed aur. E.G. Bowen in *The Settlements of the Celtic Saints in Wales* tells how Gwynno came to found the church which bears his name:

> During the Yellow Plague of 547, the monks of the dead Illtud went for safety from West Wales to Brittany. Instead of returning to Pembrokeshire, they travelled East to Glamorgan to settle at Llantwit Major (Llanilltud Fawr in Welsh). It appears that Saint Illtud's monks were accompanied to Glamorgan by several of his disciples and associates, some of whom were Bretons, represented by Saint Canna at Llangan, Saint Crallo at Coychurch, Saint Isan at Llanishen, Saint Tyfodwg at Llandyfodwg, Ystradyfodwg and Llantrisant, Saint Curig at Porthkerry, and Saint Gwynno at Llanwynno and Llantrisant. Gwynno, though not as famous as other saints, nevertheless has a place among the great company of Saints who helped to bring Christianity to Wales.

At the outset, the church was probably constructed either of timber or of wattle and daub, and it was not until comparatively modern times that the building took on a mantle of stone. Until 1894 the church resembled a barn from the outside, with an appendage containing the chancel and a porch leading from the south wall (the last two features being incorporated in the present building). Inside, the pulpit was a three-decker and was situated on the north wall; the pews were interlocked and ran from east to west. In 1894 the church was restored in the Gothic style by Miss Olive Talbot, of Margam. A belfry and a small porch on the west wall were added. George E. Halliday was the architect for this work, and the cost of the work was met from Miss Talbot's own purse. As a result of this work, much of the historical interest of the building has been destroyed, though the church now has a much more imposing appearance, and there are still some historically important features inside. Affixed to the south wall of the nave, near the south door, there is the upper portion of a rough stone pillar. It is 13½in high, 8½in wide and 3½in thick. On it there is a crudely incised Latin ring-cross with four incised dots in the interspaces and four smaller dots (one of which is broken off) in the upper and lower spandrels. It dates from the period between the seventh and ninth centuries, and is ranked among the earliest Christian monuments of Wales.

Many famous people have lived in the parish since Eglwyswynno was first erected. Unfortunately, however, their fame lasted only a short while after their deaths. In Llanwynno lived one of the fastest runners ever known (if legend be allowed to count for anything), Gruffydd Morgan (Guto Nyth Brân), who once outran and caught a hare, who could keep up with the hounds, and who won races against horses. His tragic death in 1737, as a result of being slapped on the back by his sweetheart after winning a race, caused great grief in the parish, so much so that in 1866 a large tombstone was erected by public subscription as a new memorial on Guto's grave. This can be seen just behind the wall of the south porch.

The Brynffynnon Inn, Llanwynno, in 1890.

Mardy No. 3 and No. 4 Colliery in 1984. Maerdy derived its name from the old Maerdy farmhouse situated on the banks of the Rhondda Fechan river, northern end of the present-day Oxford Street. In 1875 contractors Messrs Robert Jones & Sons sank Mardy No. 1 Pit to the Abergorki seam and a year later, in 1876, Mardy No. 2 Pit was sunk. Top quality dry steam was produced in 1877. No. 3 Pit was opened in 1893 and No. 4 Pit opened in 1914 by Locket-Merthyr Steam Coal Company. (Photograph G. Bevan)

Mardy miners enjoying a pint following a hard day's graft in 1963. Left to right: Emrys James, Norman Jones (pipeman), Tom Jones (pipeman), Glyn 'Sharkey' Jones (fitter), Glyn Edwards (pipeman), Jackie Cow (repairer), Harry Bug (repairer), -?-, Kerrigan Jones (mechanic class 1). The National Power Loading Agreement (NPLA) commenced in 1966 and rest days started in 1968.

118

The proud return. Between March and April 1984 the miners' strike got underway and not a single man employed at Mardy Colliery broke the strike. On Saint David's Day, 1 March, 1985, it was agreed that all miners would return to work, and on Tuesday 5 March Mardy miners, families and friends marched proudly back to their colliery.

The last cage wind in the Rhondda Valley, 27 January 1991. Pictured are Nigel Piper (left) and Mike Winder. In the 1960s the colliery employed nearly 2,000 miners and the siding capacity, including No. 1 and No. 2, was 1,164 wagons. Since the beginning of coal production the mine has extracted 12.8 million tonnes of coal and developed 165 miles of underground roadways, equalling the distance from Cardiff to London. Mardy No. 3 and No. 4 Colliery, the last colliery in the Rhondda Valley, was closed on Friday 21 December 1990 by British Coal.

Maerdy Workmen's Hall in 1905. In 1881 the social meeting place was the Mardy Coffee Tavern, which had a library and reading room, but in 1905 this was replaced by the Workmen's Hall and Institute. It was the largest and most central building in the community and contained on the upper floor a large hall and balcony capable of accommodating over a thousand people. The building cost nearly £9,000 to build and contained one of the finest libraries in South Wales. At this time the village had really prospered, nearly a thousand houses had been built and the population was almost 7,000. Maerdy Hall was a landmark in the Rhondda Valleys; it provided a place where junior and senior choristers gathered several nights a week to practise in the schoolroom, plays were produced, drama festivals, bingo and competitions were held on the stage, snooker, billiards and games were held in the basement, twice-weekly dances were held in the Rainbow Room and the latest movies were shown in the upper floor. It was a hub of entertainment for the community and hosted many of the country's top showbiz acts. Maerdy Workmen's Hall closed on Friday 20 September 2002.

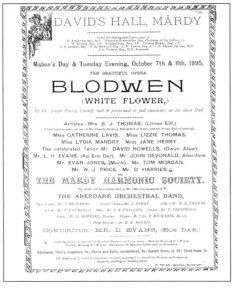

Left: Advertisement for a performance of the opera Blodwen at Saint David's Hall, Mardy, in 1895. *Right*: Mr Daniel Evans, 'Eos Dar', conductor of the Mardy Harmonic Society, established in 1882. Saint David's Hall occupied the top floor of Maerdy Hotel.

Left: D.J. Richards 1st Troop, A Squadron, 1st Reserve Cavalry Regt 5th Lancers 1918. *Right*: WAF Martha Elizabeth 'Betty' Lewis in 1940.

Left: Mr Alfred Lawes at Maerdy Cenotaph, Remembrance Day 2001. POW Alf held the Crete Veterans standard for the last time at the cenotaph and it was placed in Llandaff Cathedral on 10 July 2002. *Right*: Remembrance Day parade in 2001. The photograph includes Dennis Marsh, Brian Humphries, Dai Jones, Norman Light, Malcolm 'Pinkie' Hughes and Graham Sweet.

Maerdy huts, built in 1920.

School Street and Thomas Street VE Day celebration party, May 1945. The photograph includes Nancy Inkpen, Eirlys Jones, Ken Brown, Mrs Davies, Bopa Jones, Mrs Anne Jones, Sybil Thomas, Bopa Smith, Mary Margaret Phelps, Mr Thomas, Mair Jones, Elaine Jones, Evelyn Jones, Nan Smith, Ron Smith, Rosemary Phelps, John Inkpen, Betty Davies, Joan Davies, Thomas Davies, David Evans, Peter Brooks, Teifwen Jones, Bronfa Jones, Gwladys Jones, Vera Jones and Pauline Brooks.

Seion chapel cantata, *Snow White and the Seven Dwarves* in the vestry in 1947. The photograph includes Mr T. Rees (music conductor), Margaret and Marion Hopkins (accompanists), L. Bevan, T. Hillier, P. Brooks, J. Knight, M. Davies, M. William, M. Duggan, R. Davies, T. Grimes, B. Richards, M. Macnamarra, J. Davies, E. Davies, J. Barkway, M. Moxam, G. Williams, N. Jenkins, J. Jones, J. Pruet, E. Hillier, J. Hickman, G. Bevan, A. Newt, M. Bolton, E. Duggan, A. Fortt, A. Miles, E. Kilcoyne, H. Lewis, V. Rees, G. Chambers, M. Thomas, G. Williams, D. Rees, M. Major, J. Blake, C. Saunders, G. Morris, A. Williams and B. Jones.

Mardy Colliery cricket team 1952/53 season. Left to right, back row: Billy Davies, Emlyn Thomas, Glan Davies, Boogie Evans, Roy Thomas, Cyril Evans. Front row: Tom Howells, Gwyn Davies (wicket keeper), Owen Roberts, Jerry Blackmore (NCB director), Alan Jones, John Ivor Jones, Roy Davies.

Maerdy Square decorated with flags and bunting to welcome Her Majesty Queen Elizabeth II on the occasion of her Coronation in 1953. The population of Maerdy in 1897 was 4,752 and the village soon needed a purpose-built police station. Prior to the 1898 police station, prisoners were detained in the front room of 30 North Terrace, which had a reinforced floor to prevent the prisoners escaping.

Maerdy Central Glamorgan Brownies in 1980. Left to right, back row: Christine Thomas, Simone Evans, Diane Williams, Katherine Clements, Gail Phillips, Susan Mullins, Sarah Jefferies, Rhiân Margery, Caroline Hughes. Middle row: Siân Davies, Cerian Dorrington, Morwena Thomas (Snowy Owl), Valerie Jenkins (Brown Owl), Diane Greaves (Tawny Owl), Louise Greaves, Nicola Evans. Front row: Sharon Evans, Sarah Jones, Kristan Knott, Tara Davies, Natalie Mullins, Nicky Rossiter, Christina Harris.

Maerdy Social Club in 1995. Left to right: Howard 'Chippo' Jones, Emrys 'Babe' Carter, Bill 'Skippy' Morgan, 'Whispering Tenor', Chris Cripps. Maerdy Co-op owned the building in the 1920s; it then became an unemployed club, a boys' club and today Maerdy Social Club, which was formed in 1961 with 450 members.

Maerdy, once a small hamlet, now a proud community. It nestles in the folds of the hills of upper Cwm Rhondda Fach. Wildlife has reclaimed many of the areas from which it was temporally displaced by the industrial coal-mining past, attracted to a cleaner river and regenerating environment. This process is being aided by the Group for Environmental Awareness in Rhondda (GEAR) who received the national Queen Mother's Award in 2000 for their environmental and conservation work and the development of the Maerdy Community Woodland.

The Community School registration group 11ca, who received their records of achievement in 2001. Left to right, back row: Daniel Evans, Robbie Walters, Marc Jones, Mr Simon Keeble (teacher), David Williams, Sean Scewen, Carl Harris. Front row: Charlotte Jones, Katie Pain, Elaine Evans, Vicki Sum, Rebecca Rossiter, Laura Lewis, Mrs Elizabeth Palmer (teacher). More than 100 pupils were presented with their records of achievement at a special school assembly. The Community School opened 3 November 1969.

Maerdy Junior School year 6 in 2002. The photograph includes Aled James, Natalie Evans, Rachel Rowe, Donovan Morgan, Katie Mitchell, Dale Williams, Claire Moulding, Christian Addis, Rachel Gregory, Ashley John, Ashley Thomas, Ricky Owen, Shauna Davies, Shauna Mainwaring, Kalie Rowlands, Christopher Gordon, Sophie Price, Danielle Thomas, Shaun Curtis, Samantha Roberts, Nathan Thomas, Natalie Cole, Shaun Rogers, Stephen Jenkins, Stacey John, Stacey Mullins, Mrs J. Kucia (teacher), Mrs C. Paget (teacher), Leah Vincent, Emily Lawes, Mathew Carter, Huw Davies, Zack Llewellyn, Esther Davies, Rhian Finney, Rhys Finney and Debra Cole.

Left: Maerdy Junior School pupil Clair Evans, Welsh under-11 international footballer in 2000. Maerdy Junior School officially opened on Monday 30 June 1952. *Right*: Maerdy Elementary Girls School teachers Miss Elizabeth Mary 'Polly' Hughes and Miss Esther May Jones in 1946. Maerdy Elementary School opened on Monday 6 September 1880. Fire broke out at the school in the early hours of Monday morning 24 May 1948, completely destroying the school.

Maerdy Infant School years one and two, Saint David's Day, 1 March, 2002. Left to right, back row: Joshua Wiltshire, Levi John, Luke Hopkins, Jack Owen, Shaun Clark, Jason Lee, Liam Davies, Sam Powell. Middle row: Kaleigh Pritchard, Taylor Williams, Katie Rossiter, Laura Cooper, Demi Cole, Shauna Pritchard, Jade Hughes, Deanna Clement, Samantha Richardson, Adel Decino. Front row: Luke Mason, Tiffany Davies, Lauren Finney, Sophie Lane, Luke Hooper. Maerdy Infant School opened Monday 6 September 1880.

Cwm Rhondda

Guide me, O! Thou great Jehovah,
Pilgrim through this barren land,
I am weak, but Thou art mighty,
Hold me with Thy powerful hand;
Bread of Heaven, Bread of Heaven,
Feed me now and evermore.

Open now the crystal fountain
Whence the healing streams do flow;
Let the fiery cloudy pillar
Lead me all my journey through:
Strong Deliverer! Strong Deliverer!
Be Thou still my strength and shield.

When I tread the verge of Jordan
Bid my anxious fears subside;
Death of death, and hell's destruction,
Land me safe on Canaan's side:
Songs of praises, Songs of praises,
I will ever give to Thee.

Ten-month-old little Cwm Rhondda
Welsh lady Ellie Jay Lewis

Cwm Rhondda Christmas Memories

Christmases of my childhood in Cwm Rhondda are all rolled into one and appear in my mind like snapshots or cameo scenes in a play: the back kitchen festooned with home-made paper chains and lanterns that I'd proudly helped to make with my small fingers; my brother cracking the shells of nuts on the flagstones by crushing them with an old, black, flat iron and, as a treat, seldom-lit blazing fires in the middle kitchen and parlour with the acrid smoke filling the rooms; a stocking containing an apple, an orange and nuts hanging at the foot of the bed, presents of the *Beano*, *Dandy* and *Film Fun* annuals, a jigsaw, nurse's uniform, post office set and miniature baker, butcher and sweet shops with miniature items of merchandise; the flushed faces of friends, cousins, uncles and bopas (aunts) popping in for a drink of small beer or home-made wine and a mince pie; the gentle hissing of the gas mantle in the back kitchen; Mam making toffee apples and slab toffee and leaving the trays to cool behind the front door; in the candle glow Dad making strange and weird shadowy shapes on the wall with his hands, each of us telling ghost stories in turn; Mam telling us that she'd put extra black lead on the grate and would be leaving Welsh cakes and elderberry wine on the kitchen table for Siôn Corn (Father Christmas); whizzing down the hills past six streets on our sledges if it had snowed over Christmas; the wonderful appetizing aroma of cooking permeating the house. The tingle, rapture, thrill and excitement of the Christmases of my childhood in Cwm Rhondda and the wonderful feeling of security, warmth, togetherness and happiness which I experienced, I'll never forget.

Hawys Glyn James